EGYPT

MIDDLE EAST
REGION IN TRANSITION
EGYPT

Edited by Laura S. Etheredge, Associate Editor, Middle East Geography

Britannica® Educational Publishing
IN ASSOCIATION WITH
ROSEN
EDUCATIONAL SERVICES

Published in 2011 by Britannica Educational Publishing
(a trademark of Encyclopædia Britannica, Inc.)
in association with Rosen Educational Services, LLC
29 East 21st Street, New York, NY 10010.

Distributed exclusively by Rosen Educational Services.
For a listing of additional Britannica Educational Publishing titles, call toll free (800) 237-9932.

First Edition

Britannica Educational Publishing
Michael I. Levy: Executive Editor
J.E. Luebering: Senior Manager
Marilyn L. Barton: Senior Coordinator, Production Control
Steven Bosco: Director, Editorial Technologies
Lisa S. Braucher: Senior Producer and Data Editor
Yvette Charboneau: Senior Copy Editor
Kathy Nakamura: Manager, Media Acquisition
Laura Etheredge: Associate Editor, Middle East Geography

Rosen Educational Services
Hope Lourie Killcoyne: Senior Editor and Project Manager
Nelson Sá: Art Director
Cindy Reiman: Photography Manager
Nicole Russo: Designer
Matthew Cauli: Cover Design
Introduction by Laura Etheredge

Library of Congress Cataloging-in-Publication Data

Egypt / edited by Laura S. Etheredge.
p. cm. — (Middle East : region in transition)
"In association with Britannica Educational Publishing, Rosen Educational Services."
Includes bibliographical references and index.
ISBN 978-1-61530-325-0 (library binding)
1. Egypt. 2. Egypt—History. 3. Egypt—Politics and government.
4. Egypt—Social conditions. 5. Social change—Egypt—History. I. Etheredge, Laura.
DT46.E318 2011
962—dc22

2010025194

Manufactured in the United States of America

On the cover (clockwise from top left): A view of Cairo's skyline, featuring the 14th century Sultan Hassan Mosque; a camel caravan crosses before the pyramids of Giza; the dramatic Bibliotheca Alexandrina, inaugurated in 2002, sits near the site of the near-mythic Library of Alexandria, believed to have been destroyed nearly two millennia ago; in this copy of a painting from Queen Nefertari's tomb in Thebes, she is shown making an offering to Isis, one of the most important goddesses of ancient Egypt. © www.istockphoto.com/ TriggerPhoto; Shutterstock.com; Mohamad Al Sehety/AFP/Getty Images; Shutterstock.com

On pages 1, 14, 32, 55, 71, 90, 176, 179, 182: Cars drive on a bridge crossing the Nile on Feb. 9, 2006 in Central Cairo, Egypt. *Marco Di Lauro/Getty Images*

CONTENTS

62

72

84

128

149

159

INTRODUCTION

The ancient Greek historian Herodotus called Egypt "the gift of the Nile." Indeed, where the Nile bisects Egypt it is bordered by land of extraordinary fertility, terrain set apart in sharp relief from the aridity that marks much of the country. As this book details, the legendary generosity of the Nile provided for a large agrarian population given to the cultivation of the land, and Egypt became one of the major food producers of the region. Ideas and their exchange also flourished there, and Egypt gave rise to one of the world's earliest urban, literate societies. Readers of this comprehensive volume will learn how under a succession of local and foreign dynasties, Egypt thrived under pharaonic rule for three millennia and, with its conquest by Alexander the Great in 323 BCE, Egypt was ushered into the Hellenic world. After being taken by the Romans nearly 300 years later, it was absorbed first into that empire and subsequently into the Byzantine Empire, the successor to the Romans, before the arrival of Arab forces in the mid-7th century.

The most famous of Egypt's physical features is the Nile River. The world's longest river, the Nile dominates the topography of the country. The river runs northward on its course and, near Cairo, it begins to fan out into its delta. The Nile and its delta, along with the Western and Eastern deserts and the Sinai Peninsula, form Egypt's four major geographic regions. In a country that is mainly desert, the Eastern and Western deserts comprise some one-fourth and two-thirds of the country respectively. By contrast, both the Nile valley and Nile delta are under perennial irrigation, and agriculture is important there. In the northeast, the wedge-shaped Sinai Peninsula is

Egyptian sailboats known as feluccas, seen here on the outskirts of Cairo, are used to ferry passengers from one side of the Nile River to the other (May 2010). Khaled Desouki/AFP/Getty Images

lined by the Mediterranean Sea and the gulfs of Suez and Aqaba; in the Sinai's mountainous south lies Mount Catherine, Egypt's highest point. Egypt's climate consists of what are effectively two seasons: a cool, mild winter and a hot summer, with short transitional periods in between. Precipitation levels, low overall, decrease farther southward.

Egyptians living in the Nile valley and delta are generally an ethnically homogeneous blend of African and Arab elements. Nubians, in the extreme south of the country, differ in ethnicity and culture from other Egyptians and share similarities with groups in sub-Saharan Africa. Nomadic, semi-nomadic, and sedentary but once nomadic groups live in parts of the Sinai and in the country's deserts. Some form of Arabic—the country's official language—is spoken by most Egyptians, and the country is largely Sunni Muslim. The Christian minority is dominated by the Coptic denomination, whose community in Egypt predates the 7th century arrival of Islam. Much of Egypt's population is concentrated along the banks of the Nile, where the population density is among the world's highest. More than two-fifths of Egyptians live in cities, including Cairo, the capital and largest city. The population, generally young overall, is also increasing rapidly; efforts have been made since the 1960s to restrain the high birth rate.

Challenges facing the Egyptian economy include not only a rapidly growing population but finite land with which to support its citizens. Chronic underemployment has sent many Egyptians in search of jobs abroad. Arable land is an important resource, and although most of the country is desert, agricultural pursuits still employ some one-fourth of the population on a measure of arable land equivalent to only 3 percent of the country's area. Other resources include petroleum, although Egyptian production is low by regional standards, and significant natural gas deposits are known. The Nile offers enormous hydroelectric potential, although the majority of Egyptian power is produced by thermal means. Manufacturing increased dramatically in the 20th century, and the country produces chemicals, textiles, and other items. Raw materials, machinery, and chemical products, as well as foodstuffs, account for a significant proportion of Egyptian imports.

The current Egyptian constitution, which dates to the early 1970s, declares Egypt to be a democratic and socialist state with Islam as the state religion and Arabic as the national language. The president, who must be Egyptian, is the head of state and serves a six-year term. The president may hold an unlimited number of terms, though, and an election contested by multiple candidates and decided by popular vote was first held only in 2005. The independence of the judiciary is formally enshrined within the constitution.

Spending on health and welfare services increased at the end of the 20th century, and facilities have proliferated accordingly. Extending the coverage of health care services into rural areas is—and has long been—an important concern. Housing shortages in Egypt are significant, especially as internal migration has trended toward urban centres. Primary education is compulsory, and successful students can continue into preparatory and secondary stages.

Egypt is culturally oriented along lines that are both Arab and Islamic. Although social lifestyles vary between urban and rural settings, the status of the family as a pivot of universal importance in Egyptian society is a constant. Foreign influence over the years has been considerable, influencing dress, food, and art. As one of the major literary hubs of the Arab world, Egypt has contributed a number of the region's preeminent writers. Modern theatre, a relatively recent import, is also significant, and Egyptian films are watched avidly throughout the region. Egypt's architectural heritage, which spans millennia, is of especially great renown, and sports—football (soccer) in particular—are also of great cultural value.

The Arab invasion in the 7th century marks a turning point in Egyptian history and the start of a new cultural reality that was both Arab and Islamic. Arab conquest was not accompanied by a dramatic shift in status, though: Egypt remained a province within an empire, much as it had in the preceding centuries, and it continued to be both an important source of tax revenue and grain as well as a base of expansion. Egypt's administration was entrusted to a series of governors on behalf of first the Umayyad and then the ʿAbbāsid caliphs. Ruling Egypt from Baghdad—as the ʿAbbāsids did—was increasingly difficult, however. Perhaps to alleviate tribal strife occurring under Arab governors, Egypt's administration was handed over to Turkish governors, marking the rise of *mamlūk* (slave) rule. Efforts by these *mamlūks* to enhance their autonomy contributed to the destabilization of the ʿAbbāsids, a trend furthered with the rise of the Shīʿite Fāṭimid dynasty (969–1171), which presented itself as a political and religious rival to the Baghdad caliphate. As part of their effort to disseminate Ismāʿīlī Shīʿism, the Fāṭimids helped propel Cairo towards the intellectual fore by establishing al-Azhar, a centre of learning that drew thinkers from across the Islamic world.

Fāṭimid authority fractured under the pressure of political power struggles, and Egypt returned to the Sunni sphere under the Ayyūbid dynasty (1171–1250). Under the Ayyūbids, Egypt became an important challenger to the Crusader armies. The policy of assigning provinces to family members, while theoretically intended to ensure loyalty, instead led to power struggles that eventually destabilized the Ayyūbids. In his effort to protect the dynasty's independent military strength, the last of the Ayyūbid sultans resorted to increased reliance upon Turkish slave troops. Although these *mamlūks* had played political roles before, their rise to power in Egypt marked the first time that the former slaves took power as a self-perpetuating dynasty.

Ironically, Mamlūk rule in Egypt (1250–1517) marked the rise of Egypt as a major centre of Arab culture. In addition to providing a haven for Arab scholars and artisans displaced by the Mongols, the Mamlūks also commissioned important architectural projects, including mosques, madrasahs, and caravansaries. Life under the Mamlūks was poor for Christians, however, and conversion to Islam is thought to have increased in this period.

With the Ottoman defeat of the Mamlūks at Marj Dābiq in 1516–17, Egypt passed to the Ottomans and was once again a province in an empire. Economic decline, which had begun at the end of the Mamlūk era, continued under Ottoman rule. Although the Ottomans now controlled Egypt, the Mamlūks were able to successfully penetrate the bureaucracy and the armed forces, ultimately allowing them to reassert themselves at the expense of the Ottomans. By the early 18th century the Mamlūks had emerged as the dominant political power in Egypt. An Ottoman expedition sent to curb Mamlūk autonomy by force was unsuccessful, and the Mamlūks maintained power until the arrival of the French at the end of the 18th century.

Although a direct invasion of Britain was considered impossible, Napoleon hoped to strike British interests by occupying Egypt. The French invasion of Egypt was brief but politically significant: the Mamlūks were weakened, and the Ottomans—intent on reasserting themselves in Egypt—established a viceroy (ruler) and an occupying army there. These forces were dominated by an Albanian contingent that later gave rise to Muḥammad ʿAlī, who, as viceroy, was able to assert himself against the Ottomans over a reign of more than four decades. European intervention staved off Muḥammad ʿAlī's expansion, and although his empire soon crumbled, Muḥammad ʿAlī's family was granted the desirable right to hereditary rule over Egypt.

The scope of Westernization was variable under Muḥammad ʿAlī's successors. Many Westernizing policies were reversed under Abbas I (1848–54); the course was reversed again under Saʿīd (1854–63), who in 1854 granted a concession to a friend, a Frenchman, for the cutting of the Suez Canal. The rule of Ismāʿīl (1863–79) saw the magnification of Egypt's debt, which was exacerbated by Ismāʿīl's extravagant spending. Efforts to stave off bankruptcy failed, and in 1876 a commission was established to service the Egyptian debt, while Egyptian income and expenditures were to be supervised by Britain and France. The domination of Egypt was met with discontent that alarmed the European powers, and in September 1882 Britain occupied Cairo, launching a period of British domination in Egypt that would last until the mid-20th century.

Although the British perceived themselves as benefactors, many Egyptians were frustrated by British interference. Egyptian nationalists were strengthened by events such as the 1906 Dinshaway Incident, an encounter between British soldiers and Egyptian villagers that resulted in the death of a British soldier. At the start of World War I the British declared a protectorate over Egypt, but nationalist agitation led the British to declare Egyptian independence in February 1922, and Egypt became a monarchy (1922–52).

The rule of the monarchy in Egypt was a turbulent one, and by the mid-20th century, revolution was brewing. The monarchy was toppled in 1952 by a military coup led by Col. Gamal Abdel Nasser. A shift in Nasser's initially pro-Western orientation was expedited by British and U.S. refusal to provide promised funds for the construction of Egypt's Aswan High Dam. In July 1956 Nasser nationalized the Suez Canal in order to finance the project, provoking Britain and France—the canal's major shareholders—and sparking the Suez Crisis.

Nasser coupled generally moderate policy toward Israel with confrontational rhetoric to support his standing in the Arab world. Militant inaction was soon abandoned, though, and in 1967 the June (Six-Day) War was begun. Although Egypt and its allies were effectively routed, Soviet assistance enabled Egypt to rearm rapidly. Shortly thereafter it launched the lower-level conflict known as the War of Attrition (1969–70), which was meant to wear out Israel gradually.

After Nasser's death in September 1970, his vice president, Anwar el-Sādāt, ascended to power. In 1973 Sādāt launched the October (Yom Kippur) War against Israel, and although Egypt won a military victory in no sense, Sādāt was able to secure an honourable peace. Further, Sādāt saw peace with Israel as being in Egypt's best interest, and in 1977 he made the unprecedented move of addressing the Knesset in Jerusalem in an effort to secure a unilateral peace. Both Sādāt and his Israeli counterpart were awarded the Nobel Peace Prize for their roles in the negotiations, but Egypt lost the financial support of the Arab world and was expelled from the Arab League.

Sādāt instituted programs meant to improve the Egyptian economy, and the political power of Egyptian citizens was increased. However, political liberalization could not substitute for disappointment over the failure to improve the economy, and unrest persisted. Muslim extremism flourished under Sādāt, and in 1981, it was soldiers associated with Islamic Jihad who assassinated him. The subsequent rise of Hosnī Mubārāk, Sādāt's vice president, would be the defining factor in Egyptian politics for the next three decades.

Although Mubārāk's policy was initially moderate, power in Egypt continued to be coloured by authoritarianism, and Mubārāk was reelected—without opposition—through the end of the 20th century. Opponents were permitted to contest the 2005 election, but under suspicion of vote rigging, Mubārāk won that election too. Egypt under Mubārāk was freer than it had been under Nasser or Sādāt, but in 1995 Mubārāk introduced legislation allowing the prosecution of journalists critical of government officials, and human rights abuses were alleged. Muslim militants were pursued, but domestic terrorism continued to be a major threat: terrorism and assassinations threatened tourists and government officials, and in 1995 an assassination attempt was made on the president himself.

At the end of the first decade of the 21st century Mubārāk remained firmly in power. Rumours arose suggesting that the president, then in his 80s, was in ill health, and journalists reporting the rumour were persecuted. The continued prevalence of economic difficulties, questions of interfaith relations, and the issue of Islamic extremism—all explored in this comprehensive volume—suggested that these concerns would continue to influence Egyptian affairs well into the 21st century.

CHAPTER 1

LAND

Egypt's land frontiers border Libya to the west, Sudan to the south, and Israel to the northeast. In the north its Mediterranean coastline is about 620 miles (1,000 km), and in the east its coastline on the Red Sea and the Gulf of Aqaba is about 1,200 miles (1,900 km).

RELIEF

The topography of Egypt is dominated by the Nile. For about 750 miles (1,200 km) of its northward course through the country, the river cuts its way through bare desert, its narrow valley a sharply delineated strip of green, abundantly fecund in contrast to the desolation that surrounds it. From Lake Nasser, the river's entrance into southern Egypt, to Cairo in the north, the Nile is hemmed into its trenchlike valley by bordering cliffs, but at Cairo these disappear, and the river begins to fan out into its delta. The Nile and the delta form the first of four physiographic regions, the others being the Western Desert (Arabic Al-Ṣaḥrāʾ al-Gharbiyyah), the Eastern Desert (Al-Ṣaḥrāʾ al-Sharqiyyah), and the Sinai Peninsula.

The Nile divides the desert plateau through which it flows into two unequal sections—the Western Desert, between the river and the Libyan frontier, and the Eastern Desert, extending to the Suez Canal, the Gulf of Suez, and the Red Sea. Each of the two has a distinctive character, as does the third and smallest of the Egyptian deserts, the Sinai. The Western Desert (a branch of the Libyan Desert) is arid and without wadis (dry beds of seasonal rivers), while the Eastern Desert is extensively dissected by wadis and fringed by rugged mountains in the east. The desert of central Sinai is open country, broken by isolated hills and scored by wadis.

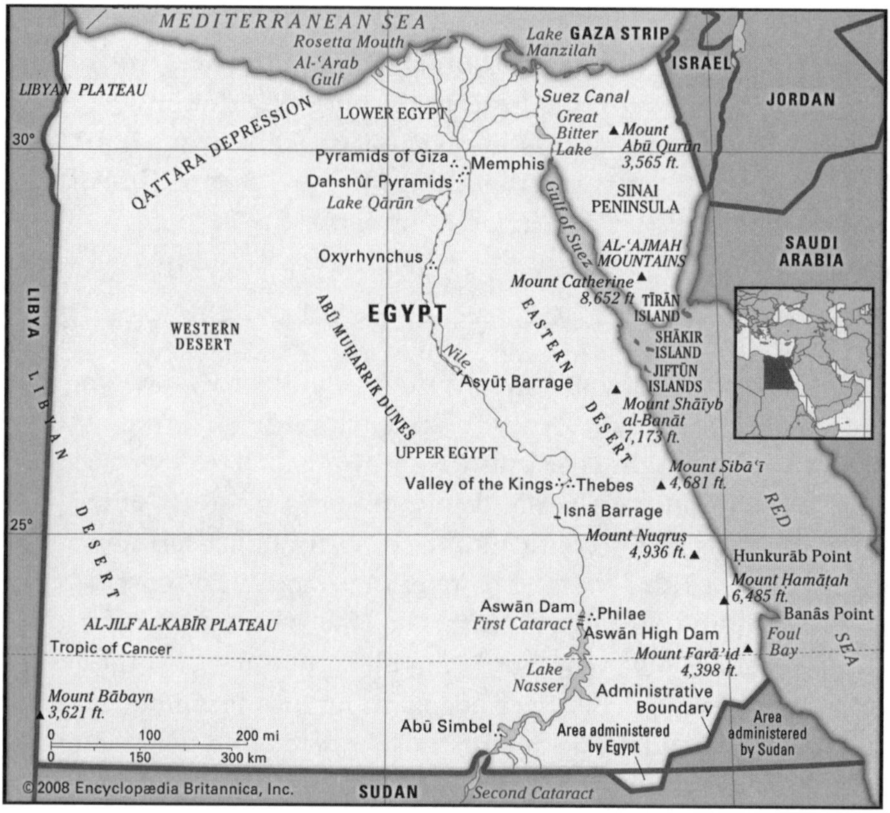

Egypt is not, as is often believed, an entirely flat country. In addition to the mountains along the Red Sea, mountainous areas occur in the extreme southwest of the Western Desert and in the southern Sinai Peninsula. The high ground in the southwest is associated with the 'Uwaynāt mountain mass, which lies just outside Egyptian territory.

The coastal regions of Egypt, with the exception of the delta, are everywhere hemmed in either by desert or by mountain; they are arid or of very limited fertility. The coastal plain in both the north and east tends to be narrow; it seldom exceeds a width of 30 miles (48 km). With the exception of the cities of Alexandria, Port Said, and Suez and a few small ports and resorts such as Marsā Maṭrūh and Al-'Alamayn (El-Alamein), the coastal regions are sparsely populated and underdeveloped.

The Nile Valley and Delta

The Nile delta, or Lower Egypt, covers an area of 9,650 square miles (25,000 square km). It is about 100 miles (160 km) long from Cairo to the Mediterranean, with a coastline stretching some 150 miles (240 km) from Alexandria to Port Said. As many as seven branches of the river once flowed through the delta, but its waters are now concentrated in two, the Damietta Branch to the east and the Rosetta Branch to the west. Though totally flat apart from an occasional mound projecting through the alluvium, the delta is far from featureless; it is crisscrossed by a maze of canals and drainage channels. Much of the delta coast is taken up by the brackish lagoons of lakes Maryūṭ, Idkū, Burullus, and Manzala (Buḥayrat al-Manzilah). The conversion of the delta to perennial irrigation has made possible the raising of two or three crops a year, instead of one, over more than half of its total area.

The cultivated portion of the Nile valley between Cairo and Aswān varies from 5 to 10 miles (8 to 16 km) in width, although there are places where it narrows to a few hundred yards and others where it broadens to 14 miles (23 km). Since the completion of the Aswan High Dam in 1970, the 3,900-square mile (10,100 square km) valley has been under repeated irrigation.

Until it was flooded by the waters impounded behind the High Dam to form Lake Nasser, the Nubian valley of the Nile extended for 160 miles (250 km) between the town of Aswān and the Sudanese border—a narrow and picturesque gorge with a limited cultivable area. The

100,000 or so inhabitants were resettled, mainly in the government-built villages of New Nubia, at Kawm Umbū (Kom Ombo), north of Aswān. Lake Nasser was developed during the 1970s for its fishing and as a tourist area, and settlements have grown up around it.

The Eastern Desert

The Eastern Desert comprises almost one-fourth of the land surface of Egypt and covers an area of about 85,690 square miles (221,900 square km). The northern tier is a limestone plateau consisting of rolling hills, stretching from the Mediterranean coastal plain to a point roughly opposite Qinā on the Nile. Near Qinā, the plateau breaks up into cliffs about 1,600 feet (500 metres) high and is deeply scored by wadis, which make the terrain very difficult to traverse. The outlets of some of the main wadis form deep bays, which contain small settlements of seminomads. The second tier includes the sandstone plateau from Qinā southward. The plateau is also deeply indented by ravines, but they are relatively free from obstacles, and some are usable as routes. The third tier consists of the Red Sea Hills and the Red Sea coastal plain. The hills run from near Suez to the Sudanese border; they are not a continuous range but consist of a series of interlocking systems more or less in alignment. A number of peaks in the Red Sea Hills rise to more than 6,000 feet (1,800 metres), and the highest, Mount Shāʿib al-Banāt, reaches 7,175 feet (2,187 metres). They are geologically complex, with ancient igneous and metamorphic rocks. These include granite that, in the neighbourhood of Aswān, extends across the Nile valley to form the First Cataract—that is, the first set of rapids on the river. At the foot of the Red Sea Hills the narrow coastal plain widens southward, and parallel to the shore there are almost continuous coral reefs. In popular conception and usage, the Red Sea coastal area can be regarded as a subregion in itself.

The Western Desert

The Western Desert comprises two-thirds of the land surface of Egypt and covers an area of about 262,800 square miles (680,650 square km). From its highest elevation—more than 3,300 feet (1,000 metres)—on the plateau of Al-Jilf al-Kabīr in the southwest, the rocky plateau slopes gradually northeastward to the first of the depressions that are a characteristic feature of the Western Desert—that containing the oases of Al-Khārijah and Al-Dākhilah. Farther north are the oases of Al-Farāfirah

Moving sands in the Sahara near Al-Jadīdah, Egypt. Georg Gerster/Photo Researchers

and Al-Baḥriyyah. Northwestward from the latter the plateau continues to fall toward the Qattara Depression (Munkhafaḍ al-Qaṭṭārah), which is uninhabited and virtually impassable by modern vehicles. West of the Qattara Depression and near the Libyan border is the largest and most populous oasis, that of Siwa. It has been inhabited for thousands of years and is relatively uninfluenced by modern development. South of the Qattara Depression, and extending west to the Libyan border, the Western Desert is composed of great ridges of blown sand interspersed with stony tracts. Beyond the Qattara Depression northward, the edge of the plateau follows the Mediterranean Sea, leaving a narrow coastal plain.

Sinai Peninsula

The Sinai Peninsula comprises a wedge-shaped block of territory with its base along the Mediterranean Sea coast and its apex bounded by the gulfs of Suez and Aqaba; it covers an area of approximately 23,000 square miles (59,600 square km). Its southern portion consists of rugged, sharply serrated mountains. These reach elevations of more than 8,000 feet (2,400 metres); among them is Mount Catherine (Jabal Kātrīnā), Egypt's highest mountain, which has an elevation of 8,652 feet (2,637 metres). The central area of Sinai consists of two plateaus, Al-Tīh and Al-'Ajmah, both deeply indented and dipping northward toward Wadi al-'Arīsh. Toward the Mediterranean Sea, the northward plateau slope is broken by dome-shaped hills; between them and the coast are long, parallel lines of dunes, some of which are more than 300 feet (100 metres) high. The most striking feature of the coast itself is a salt lagoon, Lake Bardawīl, which stretches for some 60 miles (95 km).

DRAINAGE

Apart from the Nile, the only natural perennial surface drainage consists of a few small streams in the mountains of the southern Sinai Peninsula. Most of the valleys of the Eastern Desert drain westward to the Nile. They are eroded by water but normally dry; only after heavy rainstorms in the Red Sea Hills do they carry torrents. The shorter valleys on the eastern flank of the Red Sea Hills drain toward the Red Sea; they, too, are normally dry. Drainage in the mountains of the Sinai Peninsula is toward the gulfs of Suez and Aqaba; as in the Red Sea Hills, torrent action has produced valleys that are deeply eroded and normally dry.

The central plateau of the Sinai drains northward toward Wadi al-ʿArīsh, a depression in the desert that occasionally carries surface water. One of the features of the Western Desert is its aridity, as shown by the absence of drainage lines. There is, however, an extensive water table beneath the Western Desert. Where the water table comes near the surface it has been tapped by wells in some oases.

SOILS

Outside the areas of Nile silt deposits, the nature of such cultivable soil as exists depends upon the availability of the water supply and the type of rock in the area. Almost one-third of the total land surface of Egypt consists of Nubian sandstone, which extends over the southern sections of both the Eastern and Western deserts. Limestone deposits of Eocene age (i.e., some 35 to 55 million years old) cover a further one-fifth of the land surface, including central Sinai and the central portions of both the Eastern and Western deserts. The northern part of the Western Desert consists of limestone dating from the Miocene Epoch (25 to 5 million years ago). About one-eighth of the total area, notably the mountains of the Sinai, the Red Sea, and the southwest part of the Western Desert, consists of ancient igneous and metamorphic rocks.

The silt, which constitutes the present-day cultivated land in the delta and the Nile valley, has been carried down from the Ethiopian Highlands by the Nile's upper tributary system, consisting of the Blue Nile and the ʿAṭbarah rivers. The depth of the deposits ranges from more than 30 feet (10 metres) in the northern delta to about 22 feet (7 metres) at Aswān. The White Nile, which is joined by the Blue Nile at Khartoum, in Sudan, supplies important chemical constituents. The composition of the soil varies and is generally more sandy toward the edges of the cultivated area. A high clay content makes it difficult to work, and a concentration of sodium carbonate sometimes produces infertile black-alkali soils. In the north of the delta, salinization has produced the sterile soils of the so-called *barārī* ("barren") regions.

CLIMATE

Egypt lies within the North African desert belt; its general climatic characteristics, therefore, are low annual precipitation and a considerable seasonal and diurnal (daily) temperature range, with sunshine occurring throughout the year. In the desert, cyclones stir up sandstorms or dust storms, called khamsins (Arabic: "fifties," as they are said to come 50 days per year), which occur most frequently from March to June; these are caused by tropical air from the south that moves northward as a result of the extension northeastward of the low-pressure system

Blue Nile River

The Blue Nile River (Arabic: Al-Baḥr al-Azraq; Amharic: Ābay) is a headstream of the Nile River and the source of almost 70 percent of its floodwater at Khartoum. It reputedly rises as the Ābay from a spring 6,000 feet (1,800 metres) above sea level, near Lake Tana in northwestern Ethiopia. The river flows into and out of the lake, runs through a series of rapids, and then drops into a gorge. It flows through a deep canyon southeast and west around the Ch'ok'ē Mountains and then turns northwest through Sudan to join the White Nile at Khartoum. Its length is about 907 miles (1,460 km). By far the greater part of the Blue Nile's waters come from such tributaries as the Dinder and the Rahad rivers, which rise in the Ethiopian highlands. Dams at Er Roseires (Al-Ruṣayriṣ) and Sannār, in Sudan, irrigate 1,000,000 acres (400,000 hectares) in the plain of Al-Jazīrah (Gezira) between the Blue and White Nile rivers; the Sannār Dam also produces hydroelectric power.

The Blue Nile Falls, located near the source of the Blue Nile River, Ethiopia. James P. Blair/National Geographic Image Collection/Getty Images

of Sudan. A khamsin is accompanied by a sharp increase in temperature of 14 to 20 °F (8 to 11 °C), a drop in relative humidity (often to 10 percent), and thick dust; winds can reach gale force.

The climate is basically biseasonal, with winter lasting from November to March and summer from May to September, with short transitional periods intervening. The winters are cool and mild, and the summers are hot. Mean January minimum and maximum temperatures show a variation between 48 and 65 °F (9 and 18 °C) in Alexandria and 48 and 74 °F (9 and 23 °C) at Aswān. The summer months are hot throughout the country's inland, with mean midday high temperatures in June ranging from 91 °F (33 °C) at Cairo to 106 °F (41 °C) at Aswān. Egypt enjoys a very sunny climate, with some 12 hours of sunshine per day in the summer months and between 8 and 10 hours per day in winter. Extremes of temperature can occur, and prolonged winter cold spells or summer heat waves are not uncommon.

Humidity diminishes noticeably from north to south and on the desert fringes. Along the Mediterranean coast the humidity is high throughout the year, but it is highest in summer. When high humidity levels coincide with high temperatures, oppressive conditions result.

Precipitation in Egypt occurs largely in the winter months; it is meagre on average but highly variable. The amount diminishes sharply southward; the annual average at Alexandria is about 7 inches (175 mm), Cairo has about 1 inch (25 mm), and Aswān receives virtually nothing—only about 0.1 inch (2.5 mm). The Red Sea coastal plain and the Western Desert are almost without precipitation. The Sinai Peninsula receives somewhat more precipitation: the northern sector has an annual average of about 5 inches (125 mm).

PLANT AND ANIMAL LIFE

In spite of the lack of precipitation, the natural vegetation of Egypt is varied. Much of the Western Desert is totally devoid of any kind of plant life, but where some form of water exists the usual desert growth of perennials and grasses is found; the coastal strip has a rich plant life in spring. The Eastern Desert receives sparse rainfall, but it supports a varied vegetation that includes tamarisk, acacia, and *markh* (a leafless, thornless tree with bare branches and slender twigs), as well as a great variety of thorny shrubs, small succulents, and aromatic herbs. This growth is even more striking in the wadis of the Red Sea Hills and of the Sinai and in the ʿIlbah (Elba) Mountains in the southeast.

The Nile and irrigation canals and ditches support many varieties of water plants; the lotus of antiquity is to be found in drainage channels in the delta. There are more than 100 kinds of grasses, among them bamboo and esparto (*ḥalfāʾ*), a coarse, long grass growing near water. Robust perennial reeds such as the Spanish reed and the common reed are widely distributed in Lower Egypt, but the papyrus, cultivated in antiquity, is now found only in botanical gardens.

The date palm, both cultivated and subspontaneous, is found throughout the delta, in the Nile valley, and in the oases. The doum palm (*Hyphaene thebaica*; an African fan palm) is identified particularly with Upper Egypt (the southern part of the Nile valley) and the oases, although there are scattered examples elsewhere.

There are very few native trees. The Phoenician juniper is the only native conifer, although there are several cultivated conifer species. The acacia is widely distributed, as are eucalyptus and sycamore. Several species of the genus *Casuarina* (beefwood order), imported in the 19th century, are now the country's most important timber trees. Other foreign importations, such as jacaranda, royal poinciana (a tree with orange or scarlet flowers), and lebbek (*Albizia lebbek*; a leguminous tree), have become a characteristic feature of the Egyptian landscape.

Domestic animals include buffalo, camels, donkeys, sheep, and goats, the last of which are particularly noticeable in the Egyptian countryside. The animals that figure so prominently on the ancient Egyptian friezes—hippopotamuses, giraffes, and ostriches—no longer exist in Egypt; crocodiles are found only south of the Aswan High Dam. The largest wild animal is the aoudad (a type of bearded sheep), which survives in the southern fastnesses of the Western Desert. Other desert animals are the Dorcas gazelle, the fennec (a small, desert-dwelling fox), the Nubian ibex, the Egyptian hare, and two kinds of jerboa (a mouselike rodent with long hind legs for jumping). The Egyptian jackal (*Canis lupaster*) still exists, and the hyrax is found in the Sinai mountains. There are two carnivorous mammals: the Caffre cat, a small feline predator, and the ichneumon, or Egyptian mongoose. Several varieties of lizard are found, including the large monitor. Poisonous snakes include more than one species of viper; the speckled snake is found throughout the Nile valley and the Egyptian cobra (*Naje haje*) in agricultural areas. Scorpions are common in desert regions. There are numerous species of rodents. Many varieties of insects are to be found, including the locust.

Egypt is rich in birdlife. Many birds pass through in large numbers on their spring and autumn migrations; in all, there are more than 200 migrating types to be seen, as well as more than 150 resident birds. The hooded crow is a familiar resident, and the black kite is characteristic along the Nile valley and in Al-Fayyūm. Among the birds of

The fennec, characterized by a small head and large ears, is found in northern Africa and the Sinai and Arabian peninsulas. Shutterstock.com

prey are the lanner falcon and the kestrel. Lammergeiers and golden eagles live in the Eastern Desert and the Sinai Peninsula. The sacred ibis (a long-billed wading bird associated with ancient Egypt) is no longer found, but the great white egret and cattle egret appear in the Nile valley and Al-Fayyūm, as does the hoopoe (a bird with an erectile fanlike crest). Resident desert birds are a distinct category, numbering about 24 kinds.

The Nile contains about 190 varieties of fish, the most common being *bulṭī* (*Tilapia nilotica*; a coarse-scaled, spiny-finned fish) and the Nile perch. The lakes on the delta coast contain mainly *būrī* (gray mullet). Lake Qārūn in Al-Fayyūm governorate (*muḥāfaẓah*) has been stocked with *būrī* and Lake Nasser with *bulṭī*, which grow very large in its waters.

CHAPTER 2

People

Although Egyptians are predominantly Arab, populations can vary in ethnicity and cultural orientation by region. Significant settlement areas include the Nile valley and delta, where much of the population is centred; the middle Nile valley, whose populations tend to be ethnically similar to their northern neighbours; the extreme southern valley, where populations share greater similarities with groups in sub-Saharan Africa; and the desert regions and the Sinai peninsula, where some nomadic and seminomadic groups live.

ETHNIC GROUPS

The population of the Nile valley and the delta, which are home to the overwhelming majority of Egyptians, forms a fairly homogeneous group whose dominant physical characteristics are the result of the mixing of the indigenous African population with those of Arab ancestry. Within urban areas (the northern delta towns especially), foreign invaders and immigrants—Persians, Romans, Greeks, Crusaders, Turks, and Circassians—long ago left behind a more heterogeneous mixture of physical types. Blond and red hair, blue eyes, and lighter complexions are more common there than in the rural areas of the delta, where peasant agriculturists, the fellahin, have been less affected by intermarriage with outside groups.

The inhabitants of what is termed the middle Nile valley—roughly the area from Cairo to Aswān—are known as the Saʿīdī (Upper Egyptians). Though the Saʿīdī as a group tend to be more culturally conservative, they are ethnically similar to Lower Egyptians. In the extreme southern valley, Nubians differ culturally and ethnically from other Egyptians. Their kinship structure goes beyond lineage; they are divided into clans and broader segments, whereas among other Egyptians of the valley and of Lower Egypt only known members of the lineage are recognized as kin. Although Nubians have mixed and intermarried with members of other ethnic groups—particularly with Arabs—the dominant physical characteristics tend to be those of sub-Saharan Africa.

The deserts of Egypt contain nomadic, seminomadic, and sedentary but formerly nomadic groups, with distinct ethnic characteristics. Apart from a few tribal groups of non-Arab heritage and the mixed urban population, the inhabitants of the Sinai and the northern section of the Eastern Desert are all fairly recent immigrants from

A seminomadic camp in Al-Baḥr al-Aḥmar governorate, eastern Egypt. Kurt Scholz/Shostal Associates

Arabia, who bear some physical resemblances to Arabian Bedouin. Their social organization is tribal, each group conceiving of itself as being united by a bond of blood and as having descended from a common ancestor. Originally tent dwellers and nomadic herders, many have become seminomads or even totally sedentary, as in the northern Sinai Peninsula.

The southern section of the Eastern Desert is inhabited by the Beja, who bear a distinct resemblance to the surviving depictions of predynastic Egyptians. The Egyptian Beja are divided into two tribes—the 'Ābābdah and the Bishārīn. The 'Ābābdah occupy the Eastern Desert south of a line between Qinā and Al-Ghardaqah; there are also several groups settled along the Nile between Aswān and Qinā. The Bishārīn live mainly in Sudan, although some dwell in the 'Ilbah Mountain region, their traditional place of origin. Both the 'Ābābdah and Bishārīn people are nomadic pastoralists who tend herds of camels, goats, and sheep.

The inhabitants of the Western Desert, outside the oases, are of mixed Arab and Amazigh (Berber) descent. They are divided into two groups, the Sa'ādī (not to be confused with the Sa'īdī, Upper Egyptians) and the Mūrābiṭīn. The Sa'ādī regard themselves as descended from Banū Hilāl and Banū Sulaym, the great Arab tribes that migrated to North Africa in the 11th century. The most important and numerous of the Sa'ādī group are the Awlād 'Alī. The Mūrābiṭīn clans occupy a client status in relation to the Sa'ādī and may be descendants of the original Amazigh inhabitants of the region. Originally herders and tent dwellers, the Bedouin of the Western Desert have become either seminomadic or totally sedentary. They are not localized by clan, and members of a single group may be widely dispersed.

The original inhabitants of the oases of the Western Desert were Amazigh. Many peoples have since mixed with them, including Egyptians from the Nile valley, Arabs, Sudanese, Turks, and, particularly in the case of Al-Khārijah, sub-Saharan Africans—for this was the point of entry into Egypt of the Darb al-Arbaʿīn (Forty Days Road), the caravan route from the Darfur region of Sudan.

In addition to the indigenous groups, there are in Egypt a number of small foreign ethnic groups. In the 19th century there was rapid growth of communities of unassimilated foreigners, mainly European, living in Egypt; these acquired a dominating influence over finance, industry, and government. In the 1920s, which was a peak period, the number of foreigners in Egypt exceeded 200,000, the largest community being the Greeks, followed by the Italians, British, and French. Since Egypt's independence (declared Feb. 28, 1922), the size of the foreign communities has been greatly reduced.

LANGUAGES

The official language of Egypt is Arabic, and most Egyptians speak one of several vernacular dialects of that language. As is the case in other Arab countries, the spoken vernacular differs greatly from the literary language. Modern literary Arabic (often called Modern Standard Arabic or *al-fuṣḥā*, "clear" Arabic), which developed out of classical or medieval Arabic, is learned only in school and is the lingua franca (common language) of educated persons throughout the Arab world. The grammar and syntax of the literary form of the language have remained substantially unchanged since the 7th century, but in other ways it has transformed in recent centuries. The modern forms of style, word sequence, and phraseology are simpler and more flexible than in Classical Arabic and are often directly derivative of English or French.

Alongside the written language, there exist various regional vernaculars and dialects of Arabic (these are termed collectively *al-ʿammiyyah*, "common" Arabic), which differ widely from the literary variant as well as from one another. Within the amorphous grouping referred to as Egyptian colloquial, a number of separate vernacular groups can be discerned, each fairly homogeneous but with further strata of variation within the group. (Variations from one locale to another are often subtle but at other times are quite profound.) One of these is the dialect of the Bedouin of the Eastern Desert and of the Sinai Peninsula; the Bedouin of the Western Desert constitute a separate dialect group. Upper Egypt has its own vernacular, markedly different from that of Cairo. The Cairo dialect is used, with variations, throughout the towns of the delta, but rural people have their own vernacular. Direct contact with foreigners over a long period has led to the incorporation of many loanwords into Cairene colloquial Arabic. (Cairo's prominence as a centre of the Arab film industry has also ensured that its dialect is widely understood throughout the Arab world.) The long contact with foreigners and the existence of foreign-language schools also explain the polyglot character of Egyptian society. Most educated Egyptians are fluent in English or French or both, in addition to Arabic.

There are also other minor linguistic groups. The Beja of the southern section of the Eastern Desert use an Afro-Asiatic language of the Cushitic branch known as To Bedawi (though some speak Tigre and many use Arabic). At Siwa Oasis in the Western Desert there are groups whose language is related (but not too closely) to the Amazigh languages of the Afro-Asiatic family. Nubians speak Eastern Sudanic languages that, although technically of the Nilo-Saharan language family, contain some Cushitic features. There are other minority linguistic groups, notably Greek, Italian, and Armenian, although they are much smaller than they once were.

At the time of the Islamic conquest, 639–642 CE, the Coptic language, a latter incarnation of the ancient Egyptian language, was the medium of both religious and everyday life for the mass of the population. By the 12th century, however, Arabic had come into common use even among Christian Copts, whose former tongue continued only as a liturgical language for the Coptic Orthodox Church.

Religion

Islam is the official religion of Egypt, and most Egyptians adhere to its Sunni branch. The country has long been a centre of Islamic scholarship, and al-Azhar University—located in Cairo—is widely considered the world's preeminent institution of Islamic learning. Likewise, many Muslims, even those outside Egypt, consider al-Azhar's sheikhs to be among the highest religious authorities in the Sunni world. The Muslim Brotherhood, a transnational religio-political organization that seeks to expand conservative Muslim values, was founded in Egypt in 1928. Sufism, a mystical movement within Islam, is also widely practiced.

Copts are far and away the largest Christian denomination in the country. In language, dress, and way of life they are indistinguishable from Muslim Egyptians; their church ritual and traditions, however, date from before the Arab conquest in the 7th century. Ever since it broke with the Eastern Church in the 5th century, the Coptic Orthodox Church has maintained its autonomy, and its beliefs and rituals have remained basically unchanged.

Man praying in the Blue Mosque in Cairo. Mathias Oppersdorff

The Copts have traditionally been associated with certain handicrafts and trades and, above all, with accountancy, banking, commerce, and the civil service. There are, however, rural communities that are wholly Coptic, as well as mixed Coptic-Muslim villages. The Copts are most numerous in the middle Nile valley governorates of Asyūṭ, Al-Minyā, and Qinā. About one-fourth of the total Coptic population lives in Cairo.

Among other religious communities are Coptic Catholic, Greek Orthodox, Greek Catholic, Armenian Orthodox and Catholic, Maronite, and Syrian Catholic churches as well as Anglicans and other Protestants. Few Jews remain in the country.

SETTLEMENT PATTERNS

Physiographically, Egypt is usually divided into four major regions—the Nile valley and delta, the Eastern Desert, the Western Desert, and the Sinai Peninsula. When both physical and cultural characteristics are considered together, however, the country may be further divided into subregions—the Nile delta, the Nile valley from Cairo to south of Aswān, the Eastern Desert and the Red Sea coast, the Sinai Peninsula, and the Western Desert and its oases.

About half of the population of the delta are peasants (fellahin)—either small landowners or labourers—living on the produce of the land. The remainder live in towns or cities, the largest of which is Cairo. As a whole, they have had greater contact with the outside world, particularly with the rest of the Middle East and with Europe, than the inhabitants of the more remote southern valley, and are generally less traditional and conservative than those in other regions of the country.

The inhabitants of the valley from Cairo up to Aswān governorate, the Ṣaʿīdīs, are more conservative than the

Coptic Orthodox Church

The Coptic Orthodox Church (also called the Coptic Orthodox Church of Alexandria) is the principal Christian church in predominantly Muslim Egypt. The people of Egypt before the Arab conquest in the 7th century identified themselves and their language in Greek as Aigyptios (Arabic *qibṭ*, Westernized as Copt). When Egyptian Muslims later ceased to call themselves Aigyptioi, the term became the distinctive name of the Christian minority. In the 19th and 20th centuries they began to call themselves Coptic Orthodox in order to distinguish themselves both from Copts who had converted to Roman Catholicism and from Eastern Orthodox, who are mostly Greek.

In the 4th and 5th centuries a theological conflict arose between the Copts and the Greek-speaking Romans, or Melchites, in Egypt. The Council of Chalcedon (451) rejected monophysite doctrine—the belief that Jesus Christ had only a divine, not a human, nature—and affirmed both his divinity and his humanity. The Melchites recognized the outcome of Chalcedon. The Coptic church, however, became one of the several Eastern churches that rejected the Christological language about the two natures of Christ agreed upon at Chalcedon. Yet while the Roman Catholic and Eastern Orthodox churches denounced these Eastern churches as monophysite heretics, the Coptic church and other pre-Chalcedonian or (since the 20th century) Oriental Orthodox churches adopted a theological position called miaphysitism. Confessing the statement by St. Cyril of Alexandria (*c.* 375–444) proclaiming the "one incarnate nature of the Word" of God, miaphysites declared that both Christ's humanity and divinity were equally present through the Incarnation in one single nature (hence the Greek prefix *mia*, "same") as the Word made flesh. Rather than denying Christ's humanity, as they were accused of doing, the Coptic and other miaphysite churches gave both his humanity and his divinity equal presence in the person of Christ.

After the Arab conquest of Egypt, the Copts ceased speaking Greek, and the language barrier added to the controversy. Various attempts at compromise by the Byzantine emperors came to naught. Later, the Arab caliphs, although they tended to favour those who adopted Islam, did not interfere much in the church's internal affairs. The *jizyah*, the tax levied upon non-Muslims living in an Islamic state, was abolished in the 18th century.

Arabic is now used in the services of the Coptic Orthodox Church for the lessons from the Bible and for many of the variable hymns; only certain short refrains that churchgoing people all understand are not in Arabic. The service books, using the liturgies attributed to St. Mark, St. Cyril of Alexandria, and St. Gregory of Nazianzus, are written in Coptic (the Bohairic dialect of Alexandria), with the Arabic text in parallel columns.

The Coptic Orthodox Church developed a democratic system of government after the 1890s. The patriarch and the 12 diocesan bishops, with the assistance of community councils in which the laity is well represented, regulate the finances of the churches and schools and the administration of the rules relating to marriage, inheritance, and other matters of personal status. When the patriarch dies, an electoral college, predominantly of laymen, selects three duly qualified monks at least 50 years of age as candidates for the office of patriarch. Among these three, the final choice is made by lot after prayer.

The highest-ranking bishop is the patriarch of Alexandria, who resides in Cairo; he is called the pope and claims apostolic authority for his office from St. Mark. The church has its own primary and secondary schools in many places in Egypt, as well as a strong Sunday-school movement for the religious education of children unable to go to Coptic schools. There is an Institute of Coptic Studies in Cairo, a theological college connected with the institute, and a Coptic museum; the teaching of the Coptic Orthodox Church has even become the basis of the syllabus used in the religious instruction of Christian children in government schools.

There are Coptic Orthodox churches in Jerusalem and in other areas of the Holy Land, built in the 19th and 20th centuries, as well as a Coptic bishopric in Khartoum, Sudan. The church also has a small presence in North America, Australia, and the United Kingdom. The Ethiopian, Armenian, and Syriac Orthodox churches are all Oriental Orthodox churches in communion with the Coptic Orthodox Church. The Oriental Orthodox churches were considered heretical for centuries by the Roman Catholic and Eastern Orthodox churches. Since the late 20th century, however, the Coptic Orthodox Church, like other Oriental Orthodox churches, has entered into dialogue with both, resolving many theological disputes and garnering recognition as being doctrinally in the mainstream of orthodox Christianity.

delta people. In some areas women still do not appear in public without a veil; family honour is of great importance, and the vendetta remains an accepted (albeit illegal) means of resolving disputes between groups. Until the building of the High Dam, the Aswān governorate was one of the poorest regions in the valley and the most remote from outside influences. It has since experienced increased economic prosperity.

The majority of the sedentary population of the Eastern Desert lives in the few towns and settlements along the coast, the largest being Ra's Ghārib. No accurate figures are available for the nomadic population, but they are believed to constitute about one-eighth of the region's total population. They belong to various tribal groups, the most important being—from north to south—the Ḥuwayṭāt, Maʿāzah, ʿAbābdah, and Bishārīn. There are more true nomads in the Eastern Desert than the Western Desert because of the greater availability of pasture and water. They live either by herding goats, sheep, or camels or by trading—mainly with mining and petroleum camps or with the fishing communities on the coast.

Outside the oases, the habitable areas of the Western Desert, mainly near the coast, are occupied by the Awlād ʿAlī tribe. Apart from small groups of camel herders in the south, the population is no longer totally nomadic. Somewhat less than half are seminomadic herdsmen; the remainder are settled and, in addition to maintaining herds of sheep and goats, pursue such activities as fruit growing, fishing, trading, and handicrafts. The Western Desert supports a much larger population than the Eastern Desert. Marsā Maṭrūḥ, an important summer resort on the Mediterranean Sea, is the only urban centre. Other scattered communities are found mainly near railway stations and along the northern cultivated strip. The oases, though geographically a part of the Western Desert, are ethnically and culturally distinct. The southern oases of Al-Khārijah and Al-Dākhilah have been developed to some extent as part of a reclamation project centred on exploiting underground water resources. Other oases include Al-Farāfirah, Al-Baḥriyyah, and Siwa.

The majority of the population in the Sinai Peninsula are Arabs, many of whom have settled around Al-ʿArīsh and in the northern coastal area, although substantial numbers in the central plateau and the Sinai mountains continue to be nomadic or seminomadic. Another concentration of sedentary population is found at Al-Qanṭarah, on the east side of the Suez Canal.

Rural Settlement

The settled Egyptian countryside, throughout the delta and the Nile valley to the High Dam, exhibits great

Al-Qaṣr, Egypt, in the oasis of Al-Dākhilah in the Western Desert. © Georg Gerster—Photo Researchers, Inc.

homogeneity, although minor variations occur from north to south.

The typical rural settlement is a compact village surrounded by intensively cultivated fields. The villages range in population from 500 to more than 10,000. They are basically similar in physical appearance and design throughout the country, except for minor local variations in building materials, design, and decoration. Date palms, sycamore and eucalyptus trees, and *Casuarina* (cassowary tree) species are common features of the landscape. Until comparatively recently, the only source of drinking water was the Nile; consequently, many of the villages are built along the banks of its canals. Some of the oldest villages are situated on mounds—a relic of the days of basin irrigation and annual flooding.

In the delta the houses, one or two stories high, are built of mud bricks plastered with mud and straw; in the southern parts of the valley more stone is used. The houses are joined to one another in a continuous row. In a typical house the windows consist of a few small round or square openings, permitting scant air or light to enter. The roofs are flat and built of layers of dried date-palm leaves, with palm-wood rafters; corn (maize) and cotton stalks, as well as dung cakes used for fuel, are stored on them. For grain storage, small cone-shaped silos of plastered mud are built on the roof and are then sealed to prevent the ravages of insects and rodents. Rooftops are also a favourite sleeping place on hot summer nights.

The houses of the poorer peasants usually consist of a narrow passageway, a bedroom, and a courtyard; part of the courtyard may be used as an enclosure for farm animals. Furniture is sparse. Ovens are made of plastered mud and are built into the wall of the courtyard or inside the house. In the larger and more prosperous villages, houses are built of burnt bricks reinforced with concrete, are more spacious, and often house members of an extended family. Furniture, running water, bathroom installations, and electricity are additional signs of prosperity.

Typical features of the smaller Egyptian village, in both the delta and the valley, are a mosque or a church, a primary school, a decorated pigeon coop, service buildings belonging to the government, and a few shops. Most of the people in the smaller villages engage in agriculture. In the larger villages, there may be some professional and semiprofessional inhabitants as well as artisans, skilled workers, and shopkeepers. Outside the larger settlements, combined service units—consisting of modern buildings enclosing the social service unit, village cooperative, health unit, and school—are still sometimes found, although most of such government establishments had been disbanded by the early 21st century. Much of the rural community has turned to similar services offered by nongovernmental Islamic organizations.

Unless situated on a highway, villages are reached by unpaved dirt roads. Inside the villages the roads consist mainly of narrow, winding footpaths. All villages generally have at least one drivable road.

The Western Desert oases are not compact villages but small, dispersed agglomerations surrounded by green patches of cultivation; they are often separated from each other by areas of sand. Al-Khārijah, for example, is the largest of five scattered villages. Traditionally, the houses in the oases were up to six stories high, made of packed mud, and clustered close together for defense. Modern houses are usually two stories high and farther apart.

Urban Settlement

Although for census purposes Egyptian towns are considered to be urban centres, some of them are actually

House in Cairo. A.A.A./FPG

overgrown villages, containing large numbers of fellahin and persons engaged in work relating to agriculture and rural enterprises. Some of the towns that acquired urban status in the second half of the 20th century continue to be largely rural, although their residents include government officials, people engaged in trade and commerce, industrial workers, technicians, and professional people. One characteristic of towns and, indeed, of the larger cities is their rural fringe. Towns and cities have grown at the expense of agricultural land, with urban dwellings and apartment buildings mushrooming haphazardly among the fields. There is little evidence of town or city planning or of adherence to building regulations; often mud village houses are embraced within the confines of a city.

Buildings in towns and smaller cities are usually two-storied houses or apartment blocks of four to six stories. The better ones are lime-washed, with flat roofs and numerous balconies; other houses and buildings are often of unpainted red brick and concrete.

Some Egyptian cities, such as Cairo, Alexandria, and Aswān, have special distinguishing characteristics. Cairo is a complex and crowded metropolis, with architecture representing more than a millennium of history. Greater Cairo (including Al-Jīzah and other suburban settlements) and Alexandria, together with the most important towns along the Suez Canal—Port Said, Ismailia, and Suez—are, like most other major urban centres worldwide, modern in appearance.

DEMOGRAPHIC TRENDS

Most of Egypt's people live along the banks of the Nile River, and more than two-fifths of the population lives in urban areas. Along the Nile, the population density is one of the highest in the world, in excess of 5,000 persons per

Port Said

Port Said (Arabic: Būr Sa'īd) is a port city located in northeastern Egypt, at the northern end of the Suez Canal. The city also constitutes the bulk of the urban governorate of Būr Sa'īd.

Situated largely on man-made land, the city was founded in 1859 on a low sandy strip separating the Mediterranean from Lake Manzala. Mud and sand dredged from the harbour and huge artificial stones capable of resisting saltwater action were added to the strip; its breakwaters were completed in 1868, a year before the canal was completed. The city was named after the Ottoman viceroy Sa'īd Pasha (ruled 1854–63), who selected the site of the town. Consisting initially of a grid-pattern European quarter and a native Egyptian sector, the town early established its cosmopolitan character. The outer harbour, 570 acres (231 hectares) in area, was carefully designed so that its two protecting moles, or breakwaters, prevent coastal currents from silting up the canal. The main channel is 2.5 miles (4 km) long, flanked by open basins. To house workmen of the several huge dry docks built between 1903 and 1909, a new quarter, now named Būr Fu'ād (Port Fuad), was built opposite the city proper on the eastern shore between the canal and the eastern extension of Lake Manzala.

By the late 19th century Port Said was the world's largest coal storage station, catering almost exclusively to the Suez Canal traffic. After the standard-gauge railway from Cairo via Ismailia was completed (1904), it became Egypt's chief port after Alexandria; in addition to canal traffic, Port Said handled cotton and rice exports from the eastern delta. A frozen-seafood plant for the export trade has been added to the port's fishing facilities. The city still retains the main workshops of the canal administration. During the Sinai War of 1956, which followed Egyptian nationalization of the canal, Port Said was severely damaged by the air attacks (October 31) and landings (November 5) of French and British forces. The colossal bronze statue of Ferdinand de Lesseps, builder of the canal, which stood at the base of the western mole, was removed in 1956 after angry crowds perceived in it a symbol of European intervention in Egypt's internal affairs. Britain and France were compelled to withdraw under strong United Nations pressure, and the canal was reopened; the damages of the brief campaign were repaired, and the city's trade resumed. In the June (Six-Day) War of 1967, Israeli forces occupied the eastern bank of the canal, which then remained closed until 1975.

With the promulgation of Pres. Anwar el-Sādāt's open-door economic policy (Arabic: infitāḥ) in 1975, the city was restored, new housing was built for the returning refugees of the wars with Israel, and a tax-free industrial zone was opened. The city's industries produce textiles, clothing, glass, china, automobile batteries and tires, watches, and cosmetics. It has several gas-fired electrical generating plants, as well as computer, construction, and publishing industries. There are also port and shipyard facilities, and in 1980 a bypass north of the city on the Suez Canal opened. Port Said is served by a railroad linking it to the other canal cities and by the main railway system via Ismailia.

square mile (2,000 per square km) in a number of riverine governorates. The rapidly growing population is young, with more than one-third of the total under age 15 and some three-fifths under 30. In response to the strain put on Egypt's economy by the country's burgeoning population, a national family planning program was initiated in 1964, and by the 1990s it had succeeded in lowering the birth rate. Improvements in health care also brought the infant mortality rate well below the world average by the turn of the 21st century. Life expectancy averages about 71 years for men and about 74 years for women.

CHAPTER 3

Economy

Although the constitution of 1971 describes the economy as one based on socialism, with the people controlling all means of production, the public sector thoroughly dominated the economy for only about two decades following the revolution of 1952—prior to which time the country had a free market. Most major nationalization took place between 1961 and the early 1970s, when most important sectors of the economy either were public or were strictly controlled by the government. This included large-scale industry, communications, banking and finance, the cotton trade, foreign trade as a whole, and other sectors. During that time, private enterprise came gradually to find its scope restricted, but some room to maneuver was still left in real estate and in agriculture and, later, in the export trade. Personal income, as well as land ownership, was strictly limited by the government.

Moreover, the government, when not actually in possession of the means of production, regulated all important aspects of production and distribution. It imposed controls on agricultural prices, controlled rent, ran the internal trade, restricted foreign travel and the use of foreign exchange, and appointed and supervised the boards of directors of corporations. The government initiated projects and allocated investment.

As part of the *infitāḥ* (Arabic: "opening") economic policy adopted in the mid-1970s, some of these restrictions were relaxed in the last quarter of the 20th century, permitting greater private-sector participation in various areas. Although the everyday running of corporations is now left to their boards of directors, those boards receive instructions from public boards, and the chairmen of boards often coordinate their production policies with the appropriate state minister. The government formulates five-year plans to guide economic development. Likewise, since the early 1970s, the Egyptian government has campaigned for increased foreign investment—initially receiving financial aid from the oil-rich Arab states. Although Arab aid was suspended as a punitive measure after Egypt signed a 1979 peace treaty with Israel, the subsequent return of several Western and Japanese corporations, encouraged by the normalization of Egyptian relations with Israel, increased the potential for further foreign investment in the country. Much of the effort exerted by the government in the early 1980s was devoted to adjusting the economy to the situation resulting from the 1979 treaty. Defense expenditures were reduced, and increased allocations were made available for developing roads, bridges, oil pipelines, telephone lines, and other infrastructure. Egypt's economy began to become more resilient, primarily because of new oil and natural gas discoveries but also because Western aid increased. In the late 1990s Egypt's per capita gross domestic product (GDP) rose markedly, as the government sought to raise domestic production and foreign trade.

However, the economy has continued to face many hurdles. The general standard of living in Egypt remains rather low, and in relation to the size of its population, its economic resources are limited. Land remains its main source of natural wealth, but the amount of productive land is insufficient to support the population adequately. Increases in population have put pressure on resources, producing chronic underemployment, and many Egyptians have sought employment abroad.

AGRICULTURE AND FISHING

About 96 percent of Egypt's total area is desert. Lack of forests, permanent meadows, or pastures places a heavy burden on the available arable land, which constitutes

Infitāḥ

Infitāḥ was a program of economic liberalization initiated by Pres. Anwar el-Sādāt in the early 1970s. *Infitāḥ*, officially outlined in the October Paper of April 1974, represented a marked departure from the socialist framework of his predecessor, Gamal Abdel Nasser. The open-door economic program was meant to encourage capitalist investment by domestic and foreign investors, thereby invigorating Egypt's sizable and inefficient public sector. Incentives such as reduced taxes and import tariffs were offered to investors, and foreign banks were encouraged to return to Egypt.

The program was faced with a number of significant challenges. Many investors found themselves confronted with a complex bureaucracy that made doing business in Egypt difficult. Investors who did participate in the Egyptian economy as a result of *infitāḥ* frequently invested in ventures of minimized risk such as tourism or construction, often at the expense of important but less-reliable sectors such as industry. Furthermore, *infitāḥ* policies resulted in an accentuation of the country's economic disparities: while a small proportion of individuals profited from the program, for the wider Egyptian public, which enjoyed few benefits, *infitāḥ* was largely a disappointment.

only about 3 percent of the total area. This limited area, which sustains on the average 8 persons per acre (20 per hectare), is, however, highly fertile and is cropped more than once a year.

Agriculture remains an important sector of the Egyptian economy. It contributes nearly one-sixth of the GDP, employs roughly one-fourth of the labour force, and provides the country—through agricultural exports—with an important part of its foreign exchange. The rapid increase in Egypt's population prompted an intensification of cultivation almost without parallel elsewhere. Heavy capital is invested in the form of canals, drains, dams,

Farmland near Cairo, Egypt. ©Robert Holmes

water pumps, and barrages; the investment of skilled labour, commercial fertilizers, and pesticides is also great. Strict crop rotation—in addition to government controls on the allocation of area to crops, on varieties planted, on the distribution of fertilizers and pesticides, and on marketing—contributes to high agricultural yield.

Unlike the situation in comparable developing countries, Egyptian agriculture is geared overwhelmingly toward commercial rather than subsistence production. Field crops contribute some three-fourths of the total value of Egypt's agricultural production, while the rest comes from livestock products, fruits and vegetables, and other specialty crops. Egypt has two seasons of cultivation, one for winter and another for summer crops. The main summer field crop is cotton, which absorbs much of the available labour and represents a notable portion of the value of exports. Egypt is the world's principal producer of long-staple cotton (1.125 inches [2.85 cm] and longer), normally supplying about one-third of the world crop; total Egyptian cotton production, however, constitutes just a tiny fraction of the global yield.

Among other principal field crops are corn, rice, wheat, sorghum, and fava (broad) beans (*fūl*). In spite of a considerable output, the cereal production in Egypt falls short of the country's total consumption needs, so a substantial proportion of foreign exchange is spent annually on the import of cereals and milling products. Other important crops include sugarcane, tomatoes, sugar beets, potatoes, and onions. Many varieties of fruit are grown, and some, such as citrus, are exported.

Until the completion of the Aswan High Dam in 1970, the pattern of inundation and falling water, of high Nile and low Nile, established the Egyptian year and controlled

A stand of sugarcane on the west bank of the Nile River, near Dandarah, Egypt. Bob Burch/Bruce Coleman Inc.

the lives of the Egyptian farmers. Most were tied to a life on the land—from birth to death, from century to century. On the regular behaviour of the Nile rested the prosperity, the very continuity, of the land. The three seasons of the Egyptian year were even named after the land conditions produced by the river: *akhet*, the "inundation"; *peret*, the season when the land emerged from the flood; and *shomu*, the time when water was short. When the Nile behaved as expected, which most commonly was the case, life went on as normal. When the flood failed or was excessive, disaster followed.

Construction of the Aswan High Dam enabled not only control of the Nile's floods but also the reclamation of vast tracts of land for farming. The total land reclaimed as a result of the Aswan High Dam project reached more than 1,000,000 acres (400,000 hectares) by 1975, in addition to some 700,000 acres (284,000 hectares) converted from basin (one crop per year) irrigation to perennial irrigation. During the same period, however, an agricultural area almost as large was lost to industry and growing towns. Conscious of the need to both conserve and increase arable land, the Egyptian government has encouraged the establishment of new settlements in desert areas and has promoted projects to bring large areas of unproductive desert under cultivation. The New Valley project, which was begun in 1997, is slated to bring roughly 500,000 acres (200,000 hectares) under production in the southern Western Desert by pumping water from Lake Nasser through a long canal. Major construction was completed by 2003. Similar programs have been undertaken in the western delta and the Sinai Peninsula.

Egypt has been the scene of one of the most successful attempts at land reform. In 1952 a limit of 200 acres (80 hectares) was imposed on individual ownership of land, a restriction that was lowered to 100 acres (40 hectares) in

1961 and to 50 acres (20 hectares) in 1969. By 1975 less than one-eighth of the total cultivated area was held by owners with 50 acres or more. The success of Egyptian land reform is indicated by the substantial rise of land yields after 1952. This was partly the result of several complementary measures of agrarian reform, such as regulation of land tenure and rent control, that accompanied the redistribution of the land. Rent control has since been discontinued for land and new constructions but remains in effect for older real estate.

Egypt's biological resources, centred around the Nile, have long been one of its principal assets. There are no forests or any permanent vegetation of economic significance apart from the land under cultivation. Water buffalo, cattle, asses, goats, and sheep are the most important livestock. Although animal husbandry and poultry production have been promoted by the government, growth has been sluggish.

Following the construction of the Aswan High Dam, the Egyptian government encouraged the development of a fishing industry. Construction of such projects as a fish farm and fishery complex at Lake Nasser have led to a considerable increase in the number of freshwater fish and in the size of the yearly total catch. At the same time, catches of sea fish in the waters off the Nile delta have declined, because of the change in the flow and character of Nile water after the construction of the Aswan High Dam.

RESOURCES AND POWER

Compared with the physical size of the country and the level of its population, Egypt has scanty mineral resources. The search for petroleum began earlier in Egypt than elsewhere in the Middle East, and production on a small scale began as early as 1908, but it was not until the mid-1970s that significant results were achieved, notably in the Gulf of Suez and portions of the Western Desert. By the early 1980s Egypt had become an important oil producer, although total production was relatively small by Middle Eastern standards.

The bulk of Egypt's petroleum comes from the Morgan, Ramadan, and July fields (both onshore and offshore) in the Gulf of Suez, which are operated by the Gulf of Suez Petroleum Company (commonly known as Gupco), and from the Abū Rudays area of the Sinai on the Gulf of Suez. Egypt also extracts oil from fields at Al-ʿAlamayn and Razzāq in the Western Desert. Active drilling for oil, involving several international interests, including those of the United States and several European countries, has continued in both the Eastern and the Western deserts, with marked success during the 1990s and early 21st century.

In the process of searching for oil, some significant natural gas deposits have been located, including substantial deposits in the delta and in the Western Desert, as well as offshore under the Mediterranean Sea. Wells have been established in the Abū Qīr area, northeast of Alexandria. A joint Egyptian-Italian gas discovery was made in the north delta near Abū Māḍī in 1970; this was developed partly to supply a fertilizer plant and partly to fuel the industrial centres in the north and northwest delta. In 1974 Abū Māḍī became the first Egyptian gas field to begin production. Other natural gas fields are located in the Western Desert, the delta, the Mediterranean shelf, and the Gulf of Suez, and by the early 21st century natural gas production had begun to rival that of oil, both as a source for domestic consumption and as a commodity for future export.

Egypt has several oil refineries, two of which are located at Suez. The first of Egypt's twin crude pipelines, linking the Gulf of Suez to the Mediterranean Sea near

Alexandria, was opened in 1977. This Suez-Mediterranean pipeline, known as Sumed, has the capacity to transmit some 2.5 million barrels of oil per day. The Sumed pipeline was financed by a consortium of Arab countries, primarily Saudi Arabia, Kuwait, and Egypt. In 1981 a crude oil pipeline was opened to link Ra's Shukhayr, on the Red Sea coast, with the refinery at Musṭurud, north of Cairo. Additional oil pipelines link Musṭurud with Alexandria, and fields near Hurghada to terminals on the Red Sea.

Several of Egypt's major known phosphate deposits are mined at Isnā, Ḥamrāwayn, and Safājah. Coal deposits are located in the partially developed Maghārah mines in the Sinai Peninsula. Mines located in the Eastern Desert have been the primary source for manganese production since 1967, and there are also reserves of manganese on the Sinai Peninsula. Iron ore is extracted from deposits at Aswān, and development work has continued at Al-Baḥriyyah Oasis. Chromium, uranium, and gold deposits are also found in the country.

The Nile is an incomparable source of hydroelectric energy. Before the completion of the Aswan High Dam power station in 1970, only a small volume of Egyptian electricity was generated by hydropower, with thermal plants burning diesel fuel or coal being the principal producers. For several years after the High Dam station went into operation, most of the country's electricity was generated there. Its original 12 turbines have a generating capacity of about 2 million kilowatts; the Aswan II hydroelectric power station (completed 1986) has added another 270,000 kilowatts of capacity to the system. Actual power production from the High Dam has been limited, however, by the need to reconcile demands for power with the demands for irrigation water. Moreover, Egypt's booming population and growing need for energy has forced the government to construct additional thermal plants, many of them fueled by the country's abundant reserves of natural gas. Thermal plants now generate some four-fifths of the country's electricity.

MANUFACTURING

During the 20th century, manufacturing grew to be one of the largest sectors of Egypt's economy, accounting (along with mining) for some one-third of the GDP in the early 21st century. Domestic manufactures were weak from the late 19th century until about 1930 because of free trade policies that favoured importing foreign products. Motivated by the need to increase national income, to diversify the economy, and to satisfy the aspirations of nascent nationalism, the government imposed a customs tariff on foreign goods in 1930 that promoted the development of Egyptian manufactures. The Bank of Egypt also extended loans to Egyptian entrepreneurs in the 1920s and '30s to help stimulate Egyptian domestic production. A succession of companies were founded that engaged in printing, cotton ginning, transport, spinning and weaving (linen, silk, and cotton), vegetable oil extraction, and the manufacture of pharmaceuticals and rayon. Egypt was a major Allied base during World War II (1939–45) but was largely cut off from European imports; this situation further fueled the development of manufacturing, particularly of textile products.

Most large-scale manufacturing establishments were nationalized beginning in the 1950s, and emphasis was placed on developing heavy industry after a long-term trade and aid agreement was reached with the Soviet Union in 1964. Another aid agreement with the Soviets in 1970 provided for the expansion of an iron and steel complex at Ḥulwān and for the establishment of a number of power-based industries, including an aluminum complex

Aswan High Dam

The Aswan High Dam (Arabic: Al-Sadd al-ʿĀlī) is a rockfill dam across the Nile River, at Aswān, Egypt, completed in 1970 (and formally inaugurated in January 1971) at a cost of about $1 billion. The dam, 364 feet (111 metres) high, with a crest length of 12,562 feet (3,830 metres) and a volume of 57,940,000 cubic yards (44,300,000 cubic metres), impounds a reservoir, Lake Nasser, that has a gross capacity of 5.97 trillion cubic feet (169 billion cubic metres). Of the Nile's total annual discharge, some 2.6 trillion cubic feet (74 billion cubic metres) of water have been allocated by treaty between Egypt and Sudan, with about 1.96 trillion cubic feet (55.5 billion cubic metres) apportioned to Egypt and the remainder to Sudan. Lake Nasser backs up the Nile about 200 miles (320 km) in Egypt and almost 100 miles (160 km) farther upstream (south) in Sudan. Creation of the reservoir necessitated the costly relocation of the ancient Egyptian temple complex of Abu Simbel, which would otherwise have been submerged, and 90,000 Egyptian fellahin and Sudanese Nubian nomads

The Aswan High Dam, shown here in 1967 at its first watering, was completed in 1970. AFP/Getty Images

had to be relocated. Fifty thousand Egyptians were transported to the Kawm Umbū valley, 30 miles (50 km) north of Aswān, to form a new agricultural zone called Nubaria; most of the Sudanese were resettled around Khashm al-Qirbah in Sudan.

The Aswan High Dam yields enormous benefits to the economy of Egypt. For the first time in history, the annual Nile flood can be controlled. The dam impounds the floodwaters, releasing them when needed to maximize their utility on irrigated land, to water hundreds of thousands of new acres, to improve navigation both above and below Aswān, and to generate enormous amounts of electric power (the dam's 12 turbines can generate 10 billion kilowatt-hours annually). The reservoir, which has a depth of 300 feet (90 metres) and averages 14 miles (22 km) in width, supports a fishing industry.

The Aswan High Dam has produced several negative side effects, however, chief of which is a gradual decrease in the fertility and hence the productivity of Egypt's riverside agricultural lands. This is because of the dam's complete control of the Nile's annual flooding. Much of the flood and its load of rich fertilizing silt is now impounded in reservoirs and canals; the silt is thus no longer deposited by the Nile's rising waters on farmlands. Egypt's annual application of about 1 million tons of artificial fertilizers is an inadequate substitute for the 40 million tons of silt formerly deposited annually by the Nile flood.

Completed in 1902, with its crest raised in 1912 and 1933, an earlier dam 4 miles (6 km) downstream from the Aswan High Dam holds back about 174.2 billion cubic feet (4.9 billion cubic metres) of water from the tail of the Nile flood in the late autumn. Once one of the largest dams in the world, it is 7,027 feet (2,142 metres) long and is pierced by 180 sluices that formerly passed the whole Nile flood, with its heavy load of silt.

that uses power generated by the High Dam. An ammonium nitrate plant was opened in 1971, based on gases generated in the coking unit of the steel mill at Ḥulwān. There is also a nitrate fertilizer plant at Aswān.

By the beginning of the 21st century, most large manufacturing enterprises were still owned or operated by the state, although the government had begun to sell substantial holdings to the private sector. Major manufactures included chemicals of all sorts (including pharmaceuticals), food products, textiles and garments, cement and other building materials, and paper products as well as derivatives of hydrocarbons (including fuel oil, gasoline, lubricants, jet fuel, and asphalt). Iron, steel, and automobiles were of growing importance to the Egyptian economy.

FINANCE

Modern banking activities date from the mid-19th century. The Bank of Egypt opened in 1858 and the Anglo-Egyptian Bank in 1864. The French bank Crédit Lyonnais began operations in Egypt in 1866, followed by the Ottoman Bank (1867) and then other French, Italian, and Greek banks. The National Bank of Egypt (1898) and the Agricultural Bank of Egypt (1902) were founded with British capital. The first purely Egyptian Bank was the Banque Misr (1920).

From its inception the National Bank of Egypt assumed the main functions of a central bank, a status that was confirmed by law in 1951. In 1957 all English and French banks and insurance companies were nationalized and taken over by various Egyptian joint-stock companies; thereafter, all shareholders, directors, and managers of those financial institutions were bound by law to be Egyptian citizens. Banque Misr, long responsible for controlling a number of industrial companies in addition to conducting ordinary banking business, was nationalized in 1960. As of 1961 the National Bank of Egypt—which had also been nationalized in 1960—was divided into a commercial bank that maintained the original name and the Central Bank of Egypt, which functioned as a central bank. Later that year, all remaining financial institutions were nationalized, and their operations were concentrated in five commercial banks, in addition to the central bank, the government-sponsored Public Organization for Agricultural Credits and Co-operatives, the Development Industrial Bank, and three mortgage banks. The national currency, the Egyptian pound (Arabic: *ginīh*), is issued by the central bank.

The government again reorganized the banking system in the early 1970s, merging some of the major banks and assigning special functions to each of the rest. Two new banks were created, and foreign banks were again permitted in the country as part of a program aimed at liberalizing the economy. Of particular interest were joint banking ventures between Egyptian and foreign banks. In 1980 Egypt's first international bank since the revolution nearly three decades earlier was opened and a national investment bank was established. Islamic banks have been set up in Egypt, paying dividends to their investors instead of interest, which is proscribed under Islamic law. In 1992 the stock exchanges at Cairo (1903) and Alexandria (1881), which had been closed since the early 1960s, were reopened, and in 1997 they were fully merged as the Cairo and Alexandria Stock Exchange.

The supply of money has, in general, followed the development of the economy; the authorities have aimed at tolerable increases in the price level, although some prices soared during the 1970s and '80s. Long pegged to the U.S. dollar, the pound was allowed to float in January 2003.

Egypt is a member of the International Monetary Fund (IMF). Since World War II the international liquidity of the Egyptian economy, including the Special Drawing Rights, added in 1970, has been depressed. In the late 1970s both internal and external debts rose, primarily because of large government subsidies to the private sector. In the 1980s and '90s the government gradually introduced price increases on goods and services, effectively reducing (though not eliminating) subsidies for food and fuel. In 1991 Egypt signed an agreement with the IMF and the World Bank called the Economic Reform and Structural Adjustment Program, which reduced the fiscal deficit, removed consumer subsidies, eliminated price controls, liberalized trade, reformed labour laws, and privatized state-owned enterprises. Although the program strengthened Egypt's economy during the 1990s, economic growth slowed in the early 21st century.

TRADE

The value of imports into Egypt is usually equal to about one-third and exports about one-tenth of the GDP. Since World War II, exports have tended to fall short of imports. The trade deficit was particularly sizable from 1960 to 1965 as expenditure on development rose, reaching a peak in 1966. After the 1973 war with Israel, there was a decided effort to restrict imports and stimulate exports, but this attempt met with little success. The trade deficit rose to record highs in the early and mid-1980s, largely because of the decline in revenue from petroleum exports and the increase in food imports. These problems have persisted in the early 21st century. The large visible trade deficit was partially offset by transfers from abroad, such as aid from Western governments and remittances from Egyptians working in other countries.

Nearly two-fifths of imports consist of raw materials, mineral and chemical products, and capital goods (machinery, electrical apparatuses, and transport equipment), some one-sixth are foodstuffs, and the remainder are other consumer goods. Roughly half of the exports by value consist of petroleum and petroleum products, followed by raw cotton, cotton yarn, and fabrics. Raw materials, mineral and chemical products, and capital goods are also exported. Among agricultural exports are rice, onions, garlic, and citrus fruit. Egypt's most important trading partners include the United States, Italy, Germany, and Saudi Arabia.

SERVICES

The service sector—including retail sales, tourism, and government services—is one of the largest in the economy. The government alone is one of the biggest employers in the country, and government contracts help fuel other sectors of Egypt's still heavily socialized economy. In spite of privatization and fiscal austerity measures in the late 20th century, construction projects, particularly major public-works projects, have been an important source of employment and a major source of national spending. Tourism has traditionally been an important source of foreign exchange, with millions visiting Egypt each year, although the number of tourists and volume of tourism revenues have fallen in times of political instability. In general, however, the number of tourists per year and the amount they spend in Egypt have risen. Most foreign visitors come from western Europe and from other Arab countries. Warm winters, beaches, and gambling casinos draw as many tourists as do Egypt's ancient monuments.

LABOUR AND TAXATION

Some one-fourth of the population derives its living from agriculture, although a growing proportion of the labour force—more than one-tenth—is engaged in manufacturing and mining. Most of the rest of the working population is employed in the service, trade, finance, and transportation sectors. Because of the shortage of land, labour underemployment began to be manifest in agriculture early in the 20th century. Since then the development of nonagricultural jobs has failed to keep pace with a rapidly growing labour force, and unemployment grew during the 1990s as the government shed large numbers of unproductive positions from the bureaucracy as part of a fiscal austerity policy. The rural population, especially landless agricultural labourers, has the lowest standard of living in the country. The salaries of professional groups are also low. Industrial and urban workers enjoy, on the whole, a higher standard. The highest wages are earned in petroleum, manufacturing, and other industries, where many workers receive additional benefits of social insurance and extra health and housing facilities. To some extent, low wages had been partly offset by the low cost of living, but since the late 1970s this advantage has been neutralized by persistent high inflation rates.

Trade unions are closely controlled by the government through the Egyptian Trade Union Federation and umbrella organizations with close ties to the government. Workers obtain a share of the profits earned by corporations and elect their representatives to company boards of directors; they are also heavily represented in the National Assembly (legislature). In all these activities, however, official selection works side by side with free elections. Trade unions are often vocally active in national policy making but are seldom the instrument for negotiating higher wages or better work conditions. Labour legislation of the early 21st century legalized some strikes, provided the union gives advance notice. However, unauthorized strikes also have taken place. There are well-defined rules regarding child labour—children as young as age 12 may work in seasonal agriculture, and children age 14 and older may engage in industrial work part-time only—but authorities have found these rules difficult to enforce. In farm families, for instance, everyone works, and even Egyptians who have left rural life may still regard children as economic assets. Discrimination based on gender is illegal, but social custom has rendered a wide variety of occupations inaccessible to women. As in some other Muslim countries, the workweek is Sunday through Thursday. Since the 1960s, several new employers' associations have arisen, and the Federation of Egyptian Industries (FEI; 1922) has regained powers it had once lost, such as the authority to reject government-proposed trade boycotts.

With the majority of the population earning very low incomes, direct taxation falls on the few wealthy; income-tax rates are made sharply progressive in an attempt to achieve a degree of equality in income distribution. Nevertheless, the income gap between rich and poor Egyptians has widened noticeably since the 1960s. Direct taxes on income, mostly levied on businesses, account for about one-fourth of governmental revenue. Sales taxes also generate about one-fourth of revenue, and customs duties (including fees from the Suez Canal) raise another one-seventh.

TRANSPORTATION AND TELECOMMUNICATIONS

Almost the entire communications system is state-controlled. It is adequate in terms of coverage, but stresses sometimes arise from excessive usage. The main patterns of transport flow reflect the topographical configuration of the country—that is to say, they follow the north-south course of the Nile, run along the narrow coastal plain of the Mediterranean Sea, and expand into a more complex system in the delta.

About four-fifths of Egypt's total road network is paved. Rural roads, made of dried mud, usually follow the lines of the irrigation canals; many of the desert roads are little more than tracks. The Cairo-Alexandria highway runs via Banhā, Ṭanṭā, and Damanhūr. The alternate desert road to Cairo from Alexandria has been extensively improved, and a good road links Alexandria with Libya by way of Marsā Maṭrūḥ on the Mediterranean coast. There are paved roads between Cairo and Al-Fayyūm, and good roads connect the various delta and Suez Canal towns. A paved road parallels the Nile from Cairo south to Aswān, and another paved road runs from Asyūṭ to Al-Khārijah and Al-Dākhilah in the Western Desert.

Cargo ship in the Suez Canal near Ismailia, Egypt. Hubertus Kauns/ SuperStock

The coastal Red Sea route to Marsā al-'Alam is poorly paved, as are the connecting sections inland.

Railways connect Cairo with Alexandria and with the delta and canal towns and also run southward to Aswān and the High Dam. Branchlines connect Cairo with Al-Fayyūm and Alexandria with Marsā Maṭrūḥ. A network of light railway lines connects the Fayyūm area and the delta villages with the main lines. Diesel-driven trains operate along the main lines; electric lines connect Cairo with the suburbs of Ḥulwān and Heliopolis. The Cairo Metro consists of two commuter rail lines, with further expansion underway.

The Suez Canal, which was closed at the time of the war with Israel in June 1967, was reopened in 1975 and was subsequently expanded to accommodate larger ships; it serves as a major link between the Mediterranean and

Feluccas (two- or three-masted lateen-rigged sailing ships) on the Nile River, near Luxor in Upper Egypt. Robert Frerck/Odyssey Productions

Red seas. The Nile and its associated navigable canals provide an important means of transportation, primarily for heavy goods. There are roughly 2,000 miles (3,200 km) of navigable waterways—about half of this total is on the Nile, which is navigable throughout its length. The inland-waterway freight fleet consists of tugs, motorized barges, towed barges, and flat-bottomed feluccas.

Blessed with a long coastline, Egypt has a number of ports, of which the busiest are Alexandria, Port Said, and Suez. Alexandria, which has a fine natural harbour, handles most of the country's imports and exports, as well as the bulk of its passenger traffic. Port Said, at the northern entrance to the Suez Canal, lacks the berthing and loading facilities of Alexandria. Suez's main function is that of an entry port for petroleum and minerals from the Egyptian Red Sea coast and for goods from Asia.

Cairo is an important communication centre for world air routes. Cairo International Airport at Heliopolis, with its second terminal building completed in 1986 and a third that began operations in 2009, is used by major international airlines, as is Nuzhah Airport at Alexandria. The national airline, EgyptAir, runs external services throughout the Middle East, as well as to Europe, North America, Africa, and the Far East; it also operates a domestic air service.

In the mid-19th century, Egypt was one of the first countries in the Middle East to establish a telegraph system, followed shortly by a telephone system. Since that time, Egypt has been a regional leader in the telecommunications field. The telecommunications infrastructure is better developed in urban areas, especially in Lower Egypt; in addition, the government has dedicated extensive resources to upgrading it. Land line density is relatively high, but the use of cellular phones, introduced in the mid-1990s, surpassed that of land lines within a decade.

Suez Canal

The Suez Canal (Arabic: Qanāt al-Suways) is a sea-level waterway running north-south across the Isthmus of Suez in Egypt to connect the Mediterranean and the Red seas. The canal separates the African continent from Asia, and it provides the shortest maritime route between Europe and the lands lying around the Indian and western Pacific oceans. It is one of the world's most heavily used shipping lanes. The canal extends 101 miles (163 km) between Port Said in the north and Suez in the south, with dredged approach channels north of Port Said into the Mediterranean, and south of Suez. The canal does not take the shortest route across the isthmus, which is only 75 miles (120 km), but utilizes several lakes, from north to south, Lake Manzala, Lake Timsah, and the Bitter Lakes: Great Bitter Lake (Al-Buḥayrah al-Murrah al-Kubrā) and Little Bitter Lake (Al-Buḥayrah al-Murrah al-Ṣughrā). The Suez Canal is an open cut, without locks, and, though extensive straight lengths occur, there are eight major bends. To the west of the canal is the low-lying delta of the Nile River; to the east is the higher, rugged, and arid Sinai Peninsula. Prior to construction of the canal (completed in 1869), the only important settlement was Suez, which in 1859 had 3,000 to 4,000 inhabitants. The rest of the towns along its banks have grown up since, with the possible exception of Al-Qanṭarah.

Ships in the Suez Canal at its opening, Nov. 17, 1869. Hulton Archive/Getty Images

State-owned Telecom Egypt has formed joint ventures with various foreign-owned companies to provide the country's cellular telephone services.

Television and radio are ubiquitous. In 1998 the government-owned Egyptian Radio and Television Union launched Egypt's first communication satellite, Nilesat, which offers access to private television broadcasters. Satellite dishes, which receive Egyptian and foreign broadcasts, are popular and relatively common among middle-class and affluent households. Internet use in Egypt is growing, and while only a small fraction of the population has direct access, many Egyptians visit Internet cafés to connect to the network. Ownership of personal computers remains limited.

Government and Society

Egypt has operated under several constitutions, both as a monarchy and, after 1952, as a republic. The first and most liberal of these was the 1923 constitution, which was promulgated just after Britain declared Egypt's independence. That document laid the political and cultural groundwork for modern Egypt, declaring it an independent sovereign Islamic state with Arabic as its language. The vote was extended to all adult males. This constitution provided for a bicameral (two-chambered) parliament, an independent judiciary, and a strong executive in the form of the king. In 1930 this constitution was replaced by another one, which gave even more powers to the king and his ministers. Following vigorous protest, it was abrogated five years later. The 1923 constitution again came into force but was permanently abolished after the revolution in 1952. The Republic of Egypt was declared in 1953. The new ruling junta—led by a charismatic army officer, Gamal Abdel Nasser—abolished all political parties, which had operated with relative freedom under the monarchy, and a new constitution, in which women were granted the franchise, was introduced in 1956. To replace the abolished political parties, the regime formed the National Union in 1957—from 1962 the Arab Socialist Union (ASU)—which dominated political life in Egypt for the next 15 years. An interim constitution was declared in 1964.

At the heart of the postrevolutionary regime was a commitment to Pan-Arabism—the nationalist philosophy that called for the establishment of a single Arab state—and during the following decades Egypt engaged in several abortive attempts to forge transnational unions with other Arab countries. In 1958 Egypt and Syria were merged into one state, called the United Arab Republic, a name that was retained by Egypt for a decade after Syria's secession in 1961. In 1971 Egypt, Libya, and Syria agreed to establish the Federation of Arab Republics, but the federation never actually materialized. A draft constitution was accepted by the heads of state of each country and was approved by referenda in each of the three member states. The capital of the federation would be Cairo. In 1977, however, deteriorating relations between Egypt and other Arab states over Egypt's peace negotiations with Israel led to the end of the federation and to Egypt's suspension from the Arab League, a regional organization of which it had been a founding member.

CONSTITUTIONAL FRAMEWORK

Egypt's current constitution was approved by referendum on Sept. 11, 1971. It proclaimed the Arab Republic of Egypt to be "a democratic, socialist state," with Islam as its state religion and Arabic as its national language. It recognized three types of ownership—public, cooperative, and private—and guaranteed the equality of all Egyptians before the law and their protection against arbitrary intervention by the state in the legal process. It also affirmed the people's rights to peaceful assembly, education, and health and social security and the right to organize into associations or unions and to vote.

According to the constitution and its subsequent amendments, the president of the republic is the head of state and, together with the cabinet, constitutes the executive authority. The president must be Egyptian, born of Egyptian parents, and at least 40 years old. The presidential term is six years and may be extended to an unlimited number of additional terms. The president has the power to appoint and dismiss one or more vice presidents, the

Pan-Arabism

Pan-Arabism is a nationalist notion of cultural and political unity among Arab countries. Its origins lie in the late 19th and early 20th centuries, when increased literacy led to a cultural and literary renaissance among Arabs of the Middle East. This contributed to political agitation and led to the independence of most Arab states from the Ottoman Empire (1918) and from the European powers (by the mid-20th century). An important event was the founding in 1943 of the Ba'th Party, which formed branches in several countries and became the ruling party in Syria and Iraq. Another was the founding of the Arab League in 1945. Pan-Arabism's most charismatic and effective proponent was Egypt's Gamal Abdel Nasser. After Nasser's death, Syria's Ḥāfiẓ al-Assad, Iraq's Ṣaddām Ḥussein, and Libya's Muammar al-Qaddafi tried to assume the mantle of Arab leadership.

prime minister (who is the head of government), ministers, and deputy ministers. In 2005 Egypt held its first presidential election where multiple candidates vied for the office and which was conducted by popular vote. Prior to that time, a single candidate had been chosen by the legislature then confirmed by national plebiscite.

The president is the supreme commander of the armed forces and has the right to grant amnesty and reduce sentence, the power to appoint civil and military officials and to dismiss them in a manner prescribed by the law, and the authority to call a referendum on matters of supreme importance. The president can, in exceptional cases and by investiture of the legislature, issue decrees having the force of law—but only for a defined time period.

Legislative power resides in the People's Assembly, which is composed primarily of elected members, some of whom must be women; a few members are appointed by the president. Members of the assembly are elected, under a complex system of proportional representation, for terms of five years. All males age 18 and older are required to vote, as well as all women on the register of voters. The president convenes and closes the sessions of the People's Assembly.

The People's Assembly must ratify all laws and examine and approve the national budget. It also approves the program of each newly appointed cabinet. Should it withdraw its confidence from any member of the cabinet, that person is required to resign. The president cannot dissolve the assembly except under special circumstances and only after a vote of approval by a people's referendum. Elections for a new assembly must be held within 60 days of dissolution.

A second body, the Consultative Assembly, was formed in 1980. It acts in many ways as an upper house of the legislature and may propose new amendments to the constitution, advise the president on issues of foreign policy and economic development, and conduct studies of any issues submitted to it by the president. Roughly two-thirds of the Consultative Assembly is elected. The remainder consists of presidential appointees. Members serve six-year terms.

The constitution also provides for a judiciary, independent of other authorities, whose functions and authority are governed by special legislation. The National Defence Council, presided over by the president of the republic, is responsible for matters relating to security and defense.

Local Government

Until 1960 all government administration was highly centralized, but in that year a system of local governance was established to decentralize administration and promote greater citizen participation at the local level. The 1960 Local Administration Law provides for three levels of subnational administration—*muḥāfaẓāt* (governorates; sing. *muḥāfaẓah*), *markaz* (districts or counties), and *qariyyah* (villages). The structure combines features of both local administration and local self-government. There are two councils at each administrative level: a people's council that is mostly elected and an executive council that is appointed. Although these councils exercise broad legislative powers, they are controlled by the central government.

Of the country's governorates, five—Cairo, Alexandria, Port Said, Suez, and Luxor—are cities with governorate status. Governors are appointed and can be dismissed by the president of the republic. The governor is the highest executive authority in the governorate, has administrative authority over all government personnel except judges in the governorate, and is responsible for implementing policy.

The governorate council is composed of a majority of elected members. According to law, at least half of the members of the governorate council are to be farmers and workers. In practice, however, it has not been possible to achieve this ratio, in part because farmers work long hours with little spare time to run for office, let alone attend long meetings. Moreover, many older farmers and workers do not have a high enough level of formal education to serve effectively. The town or district councils and the village councils are established on the same principles as those underlying the governorate councils.

The local councils perform a wide variety of functions in education, health, public utilities, housing, agriculture, and communications; they are also responsible for promoting the cooperative movement and for implementing parts of the national plan. Local councils obtain their funds from national revenue, a tax on real estate within the governorate, miscellaneous local taxes or fees, profits from public utilities and commercial enterprises, and national subsidies, grants, and loans.

Justice

The Egyptian constitution emphasizes the independent nature of the judiciary. There is to be no external interference with the due processes of justice. Judges are subject to no authority other than the law; they cannot be dismissed and are disciplined in the manner prescribed by law. Judges are appointed by the state, with the prior approval of the Supreme Judicial Council under the chairmanship of the president. The council is also responsible for the affairs of all judicial bodies; its composition and special functions are specified by law.

The court structure can be regarded as falling into four categories, each of which has a civil and criminal division. These courts of general jurisdiction include district tribunals, tribunals of the first instance, courts of appeal, and the Court of Cassation; the latter is the highest court of appeal and has the power to override the rulings of lower courts. Court sessions are public, except where consideration of matters of public order or decency decides otherwise. Sentence is passed in open session.

In addition, there are special courts, such as military courts and courts of public security—the latter dealing with crimes against the well-being or security of the state. The Council of State is a separate judicial body, dealing especially with administrative disputes and disciplinary actions. The Supreme Constitutional Court in Cairo is the highest court in Egypt. Its functions include judicial review of the constitutionality of laws and regulations and the resolution of judicial conflicts among the courts.

Egypt was the first Arab country to abolish the Sharīʿah (Islamic law) court system (1956); other courts dealing with religious minorities were also closed. Personal status issues—such as marriage, divorce, and inheritance—are now adjudicated by civil courts. The civil and penal codes as well as court procedure are based on French law, but these are influenced by Sharīʿah.

Political Process

After 1962 all popular participation and representation in the political process were through the Arab Socialist Union (ASU). In 1976, however, the ASU was split into three "pulpits": left, centre, and right. Other political parties soon formed and were recognized by a law adopted in June 1977. Having been eclipsed by the new political parties by 1978, the ASU was officially abolished by constitutional amendment in 1980.

The National Democratic Party (NDP), formed by Pres. Anwar el-Sādāt in 1978, serves as the official government party and holds nearly all the seats in the People's Assembly. The left-wing opposition is the National Progressive Unionist Party, joined by the Nasserist Party during the 1990s. The Liberal Socialist Labour Party is the legitimate right-wing opposition. The prerevolutionary Wafd Party has been re-formed, and the moderate religious groups have established an Islamic Alliance. Officially unrepresented are the communists, the Muslim Brotherhood, and the extreme religious groups. However, dozens of candidates who were elected as "independents" in the 2005 election for People's Assembly were actually members of the Muslim Brotherhood.

Theoretically, the Political Parties Affairs Committee must approve all new parties, but it has actually accepted and registered very few. In some cases, the Supreme Court has overriden the committee by permitting other parties to register.

SECURITY

Egypt maintains one of the largest and strongest military forces in the region. Roughly three-fourths of its overall military strength is in the army. The remainder is divided between the air force (including the air defense command) and navy. The army is equipped with large numbers of state-of-the-art main battle tanks along with field artillery and other armoured equipment. The air force has several hundred high-performance combat aircraft, and the navy has a small fleet composed mostly of coastal patrol craft, but that also includes frigates, destroyers, and submarines.

In Egypt's northern El-Alamein region, an Egyptian officer directs a tank during Bright Star, biannual joint war games involving 30,000 troops from 12 countries (2005). Khaled Desouki/AFP/Getty Images

Most importantly, the country is one of the few in the region with its own military industrial complex. Egyptian firms connected with the government manufacture light armoured vehicles and missiles (short and medium range) and assemble some of their heavy armoured vehicles under contracts with foreign firms. The officer corps has traditionally played a prominent role in politics. As part of the peace process with Israel, the United States has provided the country with large amounts of military aid. There are a number of paramilitary units, which are mostly responsible for internal security. The largest of these, the Central Security Forces (CSF), reports to the Ministry of the Interior and maintains troop strength nearly as high as the army. Much smaller are the National Guard, Border Guard Forces, and the Coast Guard. As is the case with many countries of the region, the intelligence services are ubiquitous and play an important role in internal security.

Both the military and paramilitary services rely on conscription to fill their ranks, with the service obligation for males beginning at age 18. An additional period of service in the military reserve is generally required after discharge. Living conditions, particularly for members of the CSF, are poor and pay is low. A short rebellion by members of the CSF in the mid-1980s led to several hundred deaths.

The Ministry of the Interior has direct control and supervision over all police and security functions at the governorate, district, and village levels. At the central level, the deputy minister for public security is responsible for general security, emigration, passports, port security, criminal investigation, ministerial guards, and emergency services. The deputy minister for special police is responsible for civil defense, traffic, prison administration, tourist police, and police transport and communications.

HEALTH AND WELFARE

The budget of the Ministry of Health has reflected an increasing expenditure on public-health programs, especially since the 1990s. The numbers of government health centres, beds in public hospitals, doctors, and dentists have increased significantly. An important aspect of health-care development in Egypt always has been the expansion of facilities in the rural areas. In the mid-20th century, rural people had access to health care primarily through a local facility that functioned simultaneously as a health centre, school, social-welfare unit, and agricultural extension station. By the early 21st century, hundreds of hospitals and thousands of smaller health units were serving rural communities. The quality of these facilities was often low, however, prompting many rural residents to seek treatment at Islamic health care centres, which were generally superior to those of the government.

Well-trained physicians and specialists are available in large numbers in the cities and larger towns. The medical profession has prestige, and only the better qualified students are accepted into medical schools.

Significant efforts have been made to promote preventive medicine. Compulsory vaccination against smallpox, diphtheria, tuberculosis, and poliomyelitis is enforced for all infants during their first two years. Schistosomiasis, a parasitic disease that is widespread among the rural population, presents a serious health problem. All health centres offer treatment against it, but reinfection can easily occur. Epidemics of malaria have been eliminated, but the disease still exists in endemic form, mainly in southern Egypt. Treatment for malaria is provided at all health centres, and the spraying of houses in mosquito-breeding areas is carried out regularly. Attention has also been given to the problem of tuberculosis; centres have been established in every governorate, and mass X-ray and immunization campaigns have been carried out.

The government has attempted to socialize medicine through such measures as nationalizing and controlling pharmaceutical industries, nationalizing hospitals run by private organizations and associations, and expanding health insurance. Since the 1970s, however, private hospitals and clinics have outstripped the quality of state-run facilities. A health insurance law, passed in 1964, provides for compulsory health coverage for workers in firms employing more than 100 persons, as well as for all governmental and public employees. Poorer Egyptians often seek medical care at clinics or hospitals run by Islamic groups.

HOUSING

Egypt has faced a serious urban housing shortage since World War II. The situation subsequently became aggravated by increased migration from rural to urban areas, resulting in extreme urban overcrowding. Although there is considerable concern over the housing problem, the combined efforts of both public and private sectors have struggled to meet the growing demand. Nearly three-fifths of all private investment went into residential construction during the mid-1980s. In the late 1990s, enormous resources were devoted to improving hundreds of identified slums, and nearly a score of new development areas and cities were constructed. Confounding the problem, however, was the increase in the urban population, estimated at more than two-fifths during the same period. In 2004 the available housing amounted to roughly a quarter million units, but the demand continued greatly to exceed that supply. Furthermore, many units remained vacant because they were overpriced or subject to assorted legal restrictions and other bureaucratic obstacles.

In the rural areas villagers build their own houses at little cost with the materials available; however, local contractors are forbidden by law from converting valuable topsoil into bricks. The government has experimented in aiding self-help projects with state loans. Ambitious rural housing projects have been carried out on newly reclaimed land; entire villages with all the necessary utilities have been built.

EDUCATION

At the end of the 19th century, there were only three state-sponsored secondary and nine higher schools in Egypt; the educational structure continued to be based on *maktab*s, or *kuttāb*s (schools devoted to teaching the Qur'ān), for primary education, and on madrasahs (Islamic colleges) for higher education. In 1923 a law was passed providing free compulsory education between the ages of 7 and 12, although that was not fully enforced until the early 1950s. There was a sharp increase in funding for education after World War II, and following the revolution of 1952 progress accelerated. One of the most significant features of this progress has been the spread of women's education, and there has been a sharp increase in the number of women attending university. Women are no longer confined to the home; many fields of employment, including the professions and even politics, are now open to them. A further result of the expansion of education has been the emergence of an intellectual elite and the growth of a middle class, consisting of members of the professions, government officials, and businessmen. Because of advances in the provision of education services, literacy

Teenage students in an Asyūṭ classroom. Asyūṭ is one of the largest settlements of Upper Egypt. Reza/Edit/Getty Images

rates have gradually risen; a growing two-thirds of men are literate, while the proportion for women—though increasing quickly—is still roughly half.

There are three stages of state general education—primary (six years), preparatory (three years), and secondary (three years). Primary education between ages 6 and 12 is compulsory. Pupils who are successful in examinations have the opportunity to continue their education first at the preparatory and then at the secondary level. There are two types of secondary schools, general and technical. General high schools offer a scientific, a mathematical, and a liberal arts curriculum; most technical schools are either commercial, agricultural, or industrial.

Alongside the Ministry of Education's system of general education, there is that provided by the institutes associated with al-Azhar University, centred on al-Azhar

Al-Azhar University

Al-Azhar Mosque (domed building on right), *with adjoining buildings of al-Azhar University (founded in 970).* Robert Frerck/Odyssey Productions

Al-Azhar University (Arabic: Jāmiʿat al-Azhar) is an important centre of Islamic and Arabic learning in the world, centred on the mosque of that name in the medieval quarter of Cairo. It was founded by the Shīʿite (and specifically Ismāʿīlī) Fāṭimids in 970 CE and was formally organized by 988. Its name may allude to Fāṭimah, the Prophet's daughter, known as "al-Zahrāʾ" ("the Luminous"), from whom the Fāṭimid dynasty derives its name. The format of education at al-Azhar remained relatively informal for much of its early history: initially there were no entrance requirements, no formal curriculum, and no degrees. The basic program of studies was—and still is—Islamic law, theology, and the Arabic language.

An Ismāʿīlī centre of learning, al-Azhar fell into eclipse after Egypt's conquer by Saladin, founder of the Ayyūbid dynasty and a Sunni, in the second half of the 12th century. It was revived under the Mamlūks (1250–1517), however, and continued to thrive thereafter as a centre of Sunni scholarship. It was damaged in an earthquake in the early 1300s and subsequently repaired. Additions, alterations, and renovations to its structures were undertaken at various points throughout the 14th and 15th centuries, particularly in the later Mamlūk period, when it came under direct patronage.

With the defeat of the Mamlūks in 1517, substantial architectural projects were few until the mid-18th century; in spite of this, al-Azhar's significance continued, and under Ottoman rule it held preeminent status among Egyptian institutions of learning. Opposition to the French in the late 18th century led to an uprising in 1798 centred on al-Azhar, and as a result it was bombarded by the French and temporarily closed. Nineteenth-century reform at al-Azhar owed in part to the involvement of a number of individuals, including Jamāl al-Dīn al-Afghānī, who taught at al-Azhar in the 1870s and emphasized that modern science and other subjects were not incompatible with the Qur'ān, and Muḥammad 'Abduh, who was influenced as a young intellectual by al-Afghānī and later proposed, as a member of a government committee, a number of broad measures for reforming al-Azhar. In the late 19th century, procedures, including admission requirements and examinations, were formalized, and a number of modern subjects—some of them obligatory—were introduced.

Al-Azhar was nationalized and again underwent substantial reforms in the early 1960s. Since that time, faculties such as those of medicine and engineering have been established; women were first admitted in 1962. The modern university offers a number of faculties, some of them for women, as well as regional facilities.

Mosque (founded 970) in the old quarter of Cairo. Al-Azhar has been an Islamic teaching centre for more than 1,000 years. Instruction is given at levels equivalent to those of the state schools, but in order to allow for greater emphasis on traditional Islamic subjects, the duration of training is lengthened by one year at the preparatory stage and two at the secondary. A large-scale modernization of the college-level curriculum, making it comparable to those of other state universities, has been carried out since 1961.

In the 1950s there were almost 300 foreign schools in Egypt, the majority of them French; many of these have since become, to varying degrees, Egyptianized. Pupils who attend these schools, at all levels, sit for the same state certificate examinations as those in the normal state system.

The oldest state universities are Cairo (1908), Alexandria (1942), ʿAyn Shams (1950), and Asyūṭ (1957). More universities were added to the state system during and since the 1970s. There are also several private universities, the oldest being the American University in Cairo (1919).

There are many institutes of higher learning, such as the Academy of Arts, comprising the higher institutes of ballet, cinema, theatre, Arab music, Western music, folklore, art criticism, and child care. Other institutes specialize in commerce, industry, agriculture, the arts, physical culture, social service, public health, domestic economy, and languages. Courses of study lead to a degree.

Cultural Life

In spite of the many ancient civilizations with which it has come into contact, Egypt unquestionably belongs to a social and cultural tradition that is Arab and Islamic. This tradition remains a constant factor in determining how Egyptians view both themselves and the world.

The story of the cultural development of modern Egypt is, in essence, the response of this traditional system to the intrusion, at first by conquest and later by the penetration of ideas, of an alien and technology-oriented society of the West. This response covered a broad spectrum—from the rejection of new ideas and reversion to traditionalisms through self-examination and reform to the immediate acceptance of new concepts and the values that went with them. The result has been the emergence of a cultural identity that has assimilated much that is new, while remaining distinctively Egyptian. The process is at work in all branches of contemporary culture.

CHAPTER 5

Daily Life and Social Customs

The population density of the inhabited area is such that the presence of people is obvious everywhere, even in the open countryside. In the early morning and the late afternoon, the fellahin can be seen in large numbers on the roads, going to or coming from the fields with their farm animals. During the entire day, the men, with their long tunics, or jellabas (*gallābiyyah*s), tucked up around the waist, can be seen working the land with age-old implements such as the *fās* (hoe) and *minjal* (sickle); occasionally a modern tractor is seen. In the delta older women in long black robes, younger ones in more colourful cottons, and children over age 6 help with the less strenuous tasks. In some parts of the valley, however, women over age 16 do not work in the field, and their activities are confined to

An Egyptian agricultural worker (fellah) wearing a traditional jellaba (gallibiya). ©1992 Bill Lyons

the household. They seldom appear in public except with a black muslin headdress covering their heads and faces. Young children can be seen everywhere—an omnipresent reminder of the country's high birth rate.

Lifestyles in the larger cities vary greatly from those of the countryside and are, in many ways, more akin to patterns found in urban culture worldwide. Although modesty is maintained in urban modes of dress—particularly given the tendency from the early 1980s onward for women to return to wearing the *ḥijāb* (headscarf and veil)—urban clothing styles differ only marginally from those found in many European cities. Likewise, foreign manners and values, mostly Western, have heavily influenced urban tastes in art, literature, cuisine, and other areas.

Throughout Egypt, the family remains the most important link in the social chain. In rural areas, particularly among the Sa'īdī of Upper Egypt and the Bedouin of the deserts, tribal identity is still strong, and great stock is put into blood relationships. There, where the control of the state is weakest, the vendetta is still a pervasive threat to civil order. Tribal affiliations are all but extinct in urban areas, but even there the day-to-day navigation of state bureaucracy and business relationships is commonly facilitated by extensive patronage systems linking the local family with far-reaching groups of relatives and friends.

Foreign influences on Egyptian cuisine as a whole have come mostly from other areas of the Mediterranean, including Greece, Turkey, and the Levant. Urban tastes, however, have been most heavily and diversely influenced from abroad. Rural tastes are represented by such dishes as *fūl mudammis* (*ful medmes*), consisting of slowly cooked fava beans and spices that is usually served with side dishes and bread and is widely considered the national food. Also much loved is *mulūkhiyyah*, a thick, gelatinous soup based on the leaf of the Jew's mallow (*Corchorus olitorius*) that is served with meat or fowl. *Kuftah*, a type of spiced meatball, is also common fare. Two types of bread predominate: a whole-grain flatbread known as *ʿaysh baladī* ("native bread"), and a variety from refined flour known as *ʿaysh shāmī* ("Syrian bread"). Falafel, a fried cake of legumes, is a staple throughout the region and probably originated in Egypt. Because of the country's dominant riverine culture, fish are prevalent, but they do not make up an enormous part of the diet. As in other countries of the Middle East, mutton is the most commonly consumed meat. Chicken is ubiquitous, and pigeon is extremely popular as a delicacy (with pigeon coops a common sight in many villages). Some desserts have been adapted from Turkish dishes, which can be seen in the common use of the paper-thin sheets of phyllo pastry in them. Honey is the most common sweetener, and native fruits—particularly figs and dates—are used in most puddings and other desserts. Although the consumption of alcoholic beverages is proscribed under Islam, locally brewed and fermented drinks are found, and some are imported. Coffee and tea are popular refreshments.

Egyptians celebrate a number of secular and religious holidays. The former include Labor Day, Revolution Day (1952), and Armed Forces Day. Religious holidays include the two *ʿīd*s (festivals) ʿĪd al-Aḍḥā and ʿĪd al-Fiṭr, the Prophet's birthday (*mawlid*) and Coptic Christmas (January 7).

THE ARTS

Egypt is one of the Arab world's literary centres and has produced many of modern Arabic literature's foremost writers. The impact of the West is one of the recurring themes in the modern Egyptian novel, as in Tawfīq Ḥakīm's *Bird of the East* (1943) and Yaḥyā Ḥaqqī's novella

The Lamp of Umm Hashim (1944). A further theme is that of the Egyptian countryside—depicted romantically at first, as in Muḥammad Ḥusayn Haykal's *Zaynab* (1913), and later realistically, as in 'Abd al-Raḥmān al-Sharqāwī's *The Land* (1954) and *The Peasant* (1968) and in Yūsuf Idrīs's *Al-Ḥarām* (1959; "The Forbidden"). A capacity to catch the colour of life among the urban poor is a characteristic quality of the early and middle work of Egypt's greatest modern novelist, Naguib Mahfouz (Najīb Maḥfūẓ), notably in *Midaq Alley* (1947). Mahfouz later won the Nobel Prize for Literature for *The Cairo Trilogy* (1956-57).

The modern theatre in Egypt is a European importation—the first Arabic-language plays were performed in 1870. Two dramatists, both born at the turn of the 20th century, dominated its development—Maḥmūd Taymūr and Tawfīq al-Ḥakīm. The latter, a versatile and cerebral playwright, has reflected in his themes not only the development of the modern theatre but also the cultural and social history of modern Egypt. The changes in Egyptian society are reflected in the themes adopted by younger dramatists.

With the country's low rates of literacy, electronic media have played an important role in spreading mass popular culture. Egyptian television has had a powerful influence on regional tastes, and viewers throughout the Arab world tune in to Egyptian programs. The country's most popular actors enjoy wide recognition abroad.

There is a relatively long tradition of filmmaking in Egypt dating to World War I, but it was the founding of Miṣr Studios in 1934 that stimulated the growth of the Arabic-language cinema. Modern Egyptian films are shown to audiences throughout the Arab world and are also distributed in Asian and African countries. The industry is owned privately and by the state—there are many private film-production companies, as well as the Ministry of Culture's

Egyptian General Cinema Corporation. Outside Egypt, the best-known Egyptian director is Youssef Chahine, who has directed films since 1950. Others include Salah Abu Sayf and Muhammad Khan. Actor Omar Sharif, who was well known among Western moviegoers of the 1960s and '70s, first emerged as an Egyptian film celebrity in 1954 and continued to star in Egyptian films into the 21st century. Prominent singers and composers such as Umm Kulthūm, Layla Murad, Farid al-Atrash, and Muhammad Abd al-Wahhab also earned immense sums for their movie acting. Notable films include *Flirtation of Girls* (1949), *Cairo Station* (1958), *Terrorism and the Kebab* (1993), and *Nasser 56* (1996).

Music and dance have long played an important part in Egyptian culture. Given the country's ethnic heterogeneity, traditional Egyptian musical styles are quite diverse. Yet the types of instruments found throughout the country are similar to those used elsewhere in the Middle East and North Africa. They include the *'ūd*, *qānūn* (a type of zither), *nāy* (flute), *riqq* (tambourine), and *rabāb* (type of two-string fiddle). Although much Egyptian music might suggest a minor key to the Western ear, numerous genres and repertoires employing an array of scales (or melodic frameworks) in fact yield great musical variety. Though many religious groups technically eschew music, musical traditions are ubiquitous. Muslims of the Sufi branch, for instance, are noted for their *dhikr*, communal repetition of the names of God, often with instrumental accompaniment and dancing. Especially in the rural south, the *zār* is a common purification ceremony involving singing, dancing, and playing of musical instruments. Although the muezzin's call to prayer and the recitation of the Qur'ān have obvious melodic qualities, these practices stand in a category separate from, and not to be confused with, that of music. Nevertheless, famous Qur'ān reciters frequently have mass followings similar to those of pop stars.

Contemporary Egyptian music embraces indigenous forms, traditional Arab music, and Western-style music. The revival of traditional Arab music, both vocal and instrumental, owes much to state sponsorship. The advent of musical recordings and, later, of radio and motion pictures fueled the rise of popular stars. The first of these was Sayyid Darwīsh (1892–1923). Muḥammad 'Abd al-Wahhāb (*c.* 1900–91) was one of the leading figures in the development of this genre, as both a composer and a singer. Umm Kulthūm (1904–75) was the leading female vocalist not

Singer Umm Kulthūm, c. *1956.* Howard Sochurek/Time & Life Pictures/ Getty Images

only of Egypt but also of the whole Arab world for almost 50 years. ʿAbd al-Ḥalīm Ḥāfiẓ (1929–77) had a successful career as both a singer and an actor. Western-style music has been a familiar component in Egyptian musical culture since the 19th century. Pioneers such as Yūsuf Greiss (1905–61) and Abū Bakr Khayrat (1910–63) succeeded in incorporating Arab elements into their Western-style compositions to give them a national colour.

A variety of martial dances have been practiced by groups throughout the country, particularly among Bedouin tribes, and in earlier generations, a class of female singers known as *ʿawālim* (singular *ʿālimah*, "learned") thrived in urban areas, performing in private venues and in the salons of the elite. During this same period, bawdy female street dancers known as *ghawāzī* (singular *ghāziyyah*) were seen as disreputable, yet that term today is often applied with much less disapprobation to women who practice rural dances. The art of *raqs sharqī* ("eastern dance")—or belly dancing, as it is known in the West—thrives among a class of professional dancers who entertain at weddings, birthdays, and other holidays.

A return to local lore as a source of inspiration for the arts is a generalized phenomenon in modern Egyptian culture. It has resulted in a revived interest in traditional crafts, in the collection of indigenous music, and the maintaining, with government sponsorship, of two folkloric dance ensembles—the Riḍā Troupe and the National Folk Dance Ensemble. In the visual arts the innovative and striking use of local themes gave rise to an active school of Egyptian painting and sculpture. An early product of the new aesthetic was *The Awakening of Egypt* (1928), a statue by Maḥmūd Mukhtār, which stands in front of Cairo University.

Egypt has one of the richest architectural traditions in the world, one that spans thousands of years and includes edifices from the Pharaonic, Hellenistic, Roman and Byzantine, Islamic, and European traditions. Numerous locations in the country have been designated UNESCO World Heritage sites for both their historic and architectural significance. From the ancient world, these locations include the ruins of the ancient city of Memphis and its necropolis, located south of Cairo, and adjacent pyramid fields—including the Pyramids of Giza and the stepped pyramid at Dahshūr; the city and necropolis at Thebes in Upper Egypt, including such prominent features as the nearby villages of Karnak and Luxor and the many tombs and ruins associated with the Valley of the Kings and the Valley of the Queens; and a series of monuments running from the ones at Abu Simbel to the Nile island of Philae in far southern Egypt. Sites from the Roman and Byzantine periods include the early Christian church of St. Menas (Abū Mīnā) near Alexandria and the Byzantine monastery of Saint Catherine's on Mount Sinai. From the Islamic period, the old city of Cairo—often termed Islamic Cairo—is replete with prominent mosques, citadels, madrasahs, and bathhouses and fountains.

Contemporary European influences can be seen, particularly in Alexandria and Cairo, where sections of each city's corniche are fronted by townhouses, hotels, and mansions of a distinctly European design. In all of the major cities, there are sections where such styles are dominant. Western influence can also be seen in many public buildings—particularly those from the colonial period—such as the Egyptian Museum in Cairo (1900). Ultramodern structures include the new incarnation of the ancient Library of Alexandria, Bibliotheca Alexandrina (opened 2002). There has also been a movement, beginning in the late 20th century, to combine European and Islamic architectural styles in new construction.

Pyramids of Giza

The Pyramids of Giza (Arabic: Ahrāmāt Al-Jīzah) are three 4th-dynasty (*c.* 2575–*c.* 2465 BCE) pyramids erected on a rocky plateau on the west bank of the Nile River near Al-Jīzah (Giza) in northern Egypt. In ancient times they were included among the Seven Wonders of the World. The ancient ruins of the Memphis area, including the Pyramids of Giza, Ṣaqqārah, Dahshūr, Abū Ruwaysh, and Abū Ṣīr, were collectively designated a UNESCO World Heritage site in 1979.

The designations of the pyramids—Khufu, Khafre, and Menkaure—correspond to the kings for whom they were built. The northernmost and oldest pyramid of the group was built for Khufu (Greek: Cheops), the second king of the 4th dynasty. Called the Great Pyramid, it is the largest of the three, the length of each side at the base averaging 755.75 feet (230 metres) and its original height being 481.4 feet (147 metres). The middle pyramid was built for Khafre (Greek: Chephren), the fourth of the eight kings of the 4th dynasty; the structure measures 707.75 feet (216 metres) on each side and was originally 471 feet (143 metres) high. The southernmost and last pyramid to be built was that of Menkaure (Greek: Mykerinus), the fifth king of the 4th dynasty; each side measures 356.5 feet (109 metres), and the structure's completed height was 218 feet (66 metres). All three pyramids were plundered both internally and externally in ancient and medieval times. Thus, the grave goods originally deposited in the burial chambers are missing, and the pyramids no longer reach their original heights because they have been almost entirely stripped of their outer casings of smooth white limestone; the Great Pyramid, for example, is now only 451.4 feet (138 metres) high. That of Khafre retains the outer limestone casing only at its topmost portion. Constructed near each pyramid was a mortuary temple, which was linked via a sloping causeway to a valley temple on the edge of the Nile floodplain. Also nearby were subsidiary pyramids used for the burials of other members of the royal family.

Khufu's pyramid is perhaps the most colossal single building ever erected on the planet. Its sides rise at an angle of 51°52' and are accurately oriented to the four cardinal points of the compass. The Great Pyramid's core is made of yellowish limestone blocks, the outer casing (now almost completely gone) and the inner passages are of finer

Nomad on a camel at the Pyramids of Giza, near Al-Jīzah, Egypt. Daryl Benson/Stone/Getty Images

light-coloured limestone, and the interior burial chamber is built of huge blocks of granite. Approximately 2.3 million blocks of stone were cut, transported, and assembled to create the 5.75-million-ton structure, which is a masterpiece of technical skill and engineering ability. The internal walls as well as those few outer-casing stones that still remain in place show finer joints than any other masonry constructed in ancient Egypt.

The question of how the pyramids were built has not received a wholly satisfactory answer. The most plausible one is that the Egyptians employed a sloping and encircling embankment of brick, earth, and sand, which was increased in height and in length as the pyramid rose; stone blocks were hauled up the ramp by means of sledges, rollers, and levers. According to the ancient Greek historian Herodotus, the Great Pyramid took 20 years to construct and demanded the labour of 100,000 men. This figure is believable given the assumption that these men, who were agricultural labourers, worked on the pyramids only (or primarily) while there was little work to be done in the fields—i.e., when the Nile River was in flood. By the late 20th century, however, archaeologists found evidence that a more

The Great Sphinx and the pyramid of Khafre, Giza, Egypt. Marco Di Lauro/Getty Images

limited workforce may have occupied the site on a permanent rather than a seasonal basis. It was suggested that as few as 20,000 workers, with accompanying support personnel (bakers, physicians, priests, etc.), would have been adequate for the task.

To the south of the Great Pyramid near Khafre's valley temple lies the Great Sphinx. Carved out of limestone, the Sphinx has the facial features of a man but the body of a recumbent lion; it is approximately 240 feet (73 metres) long and 66 feet (20 metres) high.

In the late 1980s and '90s, excavations in the environs of the pyramids revealed labourers' districts that included bakeries, storage areas, workshops, and the small tombs of workers and artisans. Mud sealings seem to date the workshop areas to the late 4th dynasty. The tombs range from simple mud-brick domes to more-elaborate stone monuments. Statuettes were found within some of the structures; hieroglyphic inscriptions on tomb walls occasionally identify the deceased.

CULTURAL INSTITUTIONS

The oldest secular learned academy in Egypt, the Institut d'Égypte, was founded in 1859, but its antecedents go back to the institute established by Napoleon in 1798. The Academy of the Arabic Language (1932), which was presided over by the veteran educator Ṭaha Ḥusayn, became, in terms of prestige and influence, one of the most important cultural institutions in Egypt.

Learned societies in Egypt support a wide variety of interests, including the physical and natural sciences, medicine, agriculture, the humanities, and the social sciences. The government has long been concerned with research, especially in science and technology. The National Research Centre was founded in 1947, and laboratory work in both pure and applied science began there in 1956. The Atomic Energy Organization was established the following year. The Academy of Scientific Research

Egyptian Museum

The Egyptian Museum (Arabic: Al-Matḥaf al-Miṣrī) is a museum of Egyptian antiquities in Cairo. The museum, founded in the 19th century by the French Egyptologist Auguste Mariette, houses the world's most valuable collection of its kind.

The Egyptian Museum was founded in 1858 at Būlāq, moved to Al-Jīzah (Giza), and moved to its present site in 1897–1902. It is unique in its presentation of the whole history of Egyptian civilization, especially of antiquities of the Pharaonic and Greco-Roman periods. The more than 100,000 items in the museum include some 1,700 items from the tomb of Tutankhamen, including the solid-gold mask that covered the pharaoh's head. Other treasures include reliefs, sarcophagi, papyri, funerary art and the contents of various tombs (including that of Queen Hetepheres), jewelry, ornaments of all kinds, and other objects. There is a block statue of Queen Hetepheres, one of the earliest examples of its type, and there is also a black granite sculpture of Queen Nefertiti. A sculpture of Amenhotep II shows him as the god Tenen. There are also granite figures of Queen Hatshepsut, as well as colossal figures of Amenhotep IV (Akhenaton) from Karnak. The museum also houses a small but fine collection of Fayum portraits from Hellenistic and Roman times.

Tutankhamen, funerary mask found in the king's tomb, 14th century BCE; *in the Egyptian Museum, Cairo.* Mike Lawn/ Hulton Archive/Getty Images

and Technology, the government body that oversees the work of many specialized research institutes, was inaugurated in 1971.

Most of the learned societies and research institutes have library collections of their own. In addition to large collections at the universities, the municipalities of Alexandria, Al-Manṣūrah, and Ṭanṭā maintain libraries. There is also a central public library in each governorate, with branches in small towns and service points in the villages. The Ministry of Culture is responsible for the Egyptian National Library (1870; Dār al-Kutub) and the National Archives (1954), both in Cairo, and the Public Libraries Administration. The Egyptian National Library, which has a large collection of printed materials, is also a centre for the collection and preservation of manuscripts. Construction of the new Bibliotheca Alexandrina was a joint venture between UNESCO and the Egyptian government.

The Ministry of Culture is also responsible for the Egyptian Museum (1902), the Coptic Museum (1910), and the Museum of Islamic Art (1881), all in Cairo; the Greco-Roman Museum (1892) in Alexandria; and for other institutions, including fine-arts museums such as the Mukhtār Museum (which houses the sculptures of Maḥmūd Mukhtār), the Nājī (Nagui) Museum, and the Museum of Modern Art, all in Cairo, and the Museum of Fine Arts in Alexandria.

SPORTS AND RECREATION

The sporting culture of modern Egypt traces its roots to ancient Egypt, where wrestling, weightlifting, stick fencing, and ball games were practiced for both amusement and physical training. The 1952 revolution resulted in unprecedented government investment in sports infrastructure for schools, universities, training institutes, and clubs in an effort to expand the country's international status.

Contemporary sports culture reveres prominent wrestlers, weightlifters (who have won most of Egypt's Olympic medals), boxers, and swimmers. Since the early 1980s, basketball's popularity in Egypt has risen thanks to the achievements of the men's national team, which won the African championship in 1983. Volleyball is another team sport that enjoys a wide following, and various martial arts (including judo and tae kwon do) are popular individual sports. However, football (soccer) remains the most popular sport in the country. The Cairo clubs al-Ahlī and Zamālik can attract as many as 100,000 spectators to their games, and between them the two teams have won dozens of domestic championships and continentwide trophies. The national team, the Pharaohs, was the first African representative at the World Cup (1934) and has won the African Cup of Nations a number of times since that competition began in 1957. In 2010 Egypt became the first country to win three consecutive African Cup of Nations titles.

The Egyptian Olympic Committee was founded in 1910, and an Egyptian first participated in the Summer Games in 1912. On several occasions Egypt has boycotted the Olympics for political reasons, first in 1956 (in protest over the Suez Crisis) and again in 1976 (against apartheid in South Africa) and 1980 (over the Soviet Union's invasion of Afghanistan). Egypt has not generally sent athletes to the Winter Games.

MEDIA AND PUBLISHING

Although privately owned periodicals are permitted, all newspapers and magazines in Egypt are subject to

Al-Ahlī fans cheer on their team during an African Champions League match in Cairo, May 9, 2010. Khaled Desouki/AFP/Getty Images

Al-Ahram

Al-Ahram (Arabic: "The Pyramids") is a daily newspaper published in Cairo, long regarded as Egypt's most authoritative and influential newspaper and one of the most important papers in the Arab world.

Al-Ahram was founded in Alexandria in 1875 by two Lebanese Christian brothers, Salīm and Bishārah Taqlā. It became a daily in 1881, although its presses were destroyed in the revolt led by Col. Aḥmad 'Urābī in the early 1880s. Publishing resumed in September 1882. In the late 1890s, several years after the death of his brother left Bishārah the sole owner, he moved *Al-Ahram* operations to Cairo. The paper became famous for its independence and objectivity—in spite of British censorship and control—and for its coverage of international news and nonpolitical news about Egypt and Egyptians. However, after censorship tightened as Egyptian independence neared, the paper's influence waned.

An Egyptian man reads a copy of Al-Ahram. Khaled Desouki/AFP/Getty Images

In the late 1950s *Al-Ahram* came under the influence of the Egyptian government, and, when Pres. Gamal Abdel Nasser nationalized the press in 1960, *Al-Ahram* became the de facto voice of the government. In 1957 Nasser had made his friend Muhammad Hassanein Heikal the editor of *Al-Ahram*, and Heikal's effect on the paper was profound. An eloquent editorialist and a solid journalist, Heikal built the paper's prestige, its journalistic excellence, and its makeup and technical operation to new levels. Under his leadership, the paper became the dominant daily in the Arab world. Heikal was removed as editor in 1974 when he lost the confidence of Pres. Anwar el-Sādāt, but the qualities he had built into *Al-Ahram* remained.

Over the years, contributors to *Al-Ahram* have included some of the most important political and literary elites of the day, including nationalist leaders Muṣṭafā Kāmil and Saʿd Zaghlūl and authors Ṭāhā Ḥusayn and Naguib Mahfouz (some of whose works were first printed as serials in *Al-Ahram*). English and French editions are also published, and an online edition began in 1998.

supervision through the government's Supreme Press Council. Daily newspapers include the long-established *Al-Ahram*, published in Cairo, and other Arabic-language papers, together with dailies in English and French. The government owns and operates the Egyptian Radio and Television Corporation, which provides programs in a variety of languages. Independent satellite companies began broadcasting in the 1990s. Egypt launched its first satellite toward the end of that decade, and Egyptians increasingly have watched programs of international origin. In spite of government and Islamic censorship, all sorts of arts and information are accessible through the Internet, as well as on video compact discs (VCDs) and DVDs. Cairo long has been the largest centre of publishing in the Middle East, a position increasingly challenged by Beirut and other Arab cities.

CHAPTER 6

History

In ancient times, Egypt was the home of one of the principal civilizations of the ancient Middle East and, like Mesopotamia farther east, was the site of one of the world's earliest urban and literate societies. Pharaonic Egypt thrived for some 3,000 years through a series of native dynasties that were interspersed with brief periods of foreign rule. After Alexander the Great conquered the region in 323 BCE, urban Egypt became an integral part of the Hellenistic world. Under the Greek Ptolemaic dynasty, an advanced literate society thrived in the city of Alexandria, but what is now Egypt was conquered by the Romans in 30 BCE. It remained part of the Roman Republic and Empire and then part of Rome's successor state, the Byzantine Empire, until its conquest by Arab Muslim armies in 639–642 CE.

FROM THE ISLAMIC CONQUEST TO 1250

The period of Egyptian history between the advent of Islam and Egypt's entrance into the modern period opens and closes with foreign conquests: the Arab invasion led by 'Amr ibn al-'Āṣ in 639–642 CE and the Napoleonic expedition of 1798 mark the beginning and end of the era. Within the context of Egyptian internal history alone, this era was one in which Egypt cast off the heritage of the past to embrace a new language and a new religion—in other words, a new culture. While it is true that the past was by no means immediately and completely abandoned and that many aspects of Egyptian life, especially rural life, continued virtually unchanged, it is nevertheless clear that the civilization of Islamic Egypt diverged sharply from that of the previous Greco-Roman period and was transformed under the impact of Western occupation.

The subsequent history of Egypt is therefore largely a study of the processes by which Egyptian Islamic civilization evolved, particularly the processes of Arabization and Islamization. But to confine Egyptian history to internal developments is to distort it, for during that entire period Egypt was a part of a great world empire; and within this broader context, Egypt's history is a record of its long struggle to dominate an empire—a struggle that is not without its parallels, of course, in both ancient and modern times.

Period of Arab and Turkish Governors (639–868)

The sending of a military expedition to Egypt from the caliphal capital in Medina came in a second phase of the first Arab conquests. Theretofore the conquests had been directed against lands on the northern borders of Arabia and were in the nature of raids for plunder; they had grown in scale and momentum as the Byzantine Empire and Persian Sāsānian dynasty—the two dominant political entities of the time—put up organized resistance. By 635 the Arabs had realized that in order to meet this resistance effectively they must begin the systematic occupation of enemy territory, especially Syria, where the Byzantine army was determined to halt the Arab forays.

The Arab Conquest

The Arabs defeated the Byzantines and occupied the key cities of Syria and Palestine, and they vanquished the Persian army on the eastern front in Mesopotamia and Iraq. The next obvious step was to secure Syria against a possible attack launched from the Byzantine province of Egypt. Beyond this strategic consideration, Arab historians call attention to the fact that ʿAmr ibn al-ʿĀṣ, the Arab

'Amr ibn al-'Āṣ

(d. 663, Al-Fusṭāṭ, Egypt)

'Amr ibn al-'Āṣ is recalled by history as the Arab conqueror of Egypt.

'Amr was a wealthy member of the Banū Sahm clan of the important tribe of Quraysh. He accepted Islam in 629–630 and, sent to Oman, in southeastern Arabia, by the Prophet Muhammad, he successfully completed his first mission by converting its rulers to Islam. As the leader of one of the three military forces sent to Palestine by the caliph Abū Bakr, he took part in the battles of Ajnādayn (634) and the Yarmūk River (636) and was responsible for the Muslim conquest of southwestern Palestine. He achieved lasting fame, however, for his conquest of Egypt—a campaign that, according to some sources, he undertook on his own initiative. After defeating large Byzantine forces at Heliopolis (now a suburb of Cairo) in 640 and Babylon (a Byzantine town on the site of the present Old Cairo) in 641, he entered the capital, Alexandria, in 642.

A successful general, 'Amr was also a capable government administrator and an astute politician. In Egypt he organized the system of taxation and the administration of justice and founded the garrison city of Al-Fusṭāṭ adjacent to Babylon, where he built a mosque—which still stands—bearing his name. At the Battle of Ṣiffīn (657), fought to decide the succession to the caliphate, he sided with Mu'āwiyah I, governor of Syria, against 'Alī, the fourth caliph of Islam. In the ensuing arbitration, he faithfully represented Mu'āwiyah, who rewarded him with the governorship of Egypt at the advent of the Umayyad caliphate (named for the Banū Umayyah clan of Mu'āwiyah) in 661.

general who later conquered Egypt, had visited Alexandria as a youth and had himself witnessed Egypt's enormous wealth. In spite of the obvious economic gain to be had from conquering Egypt, the caliph 'Umar I, according to some sources, showed reluctance to detach 'Amr's expedition from the Syrian army and even tried to recall the mission once it had embarked; but 'Amr, with or without the caliph's permission, undertook the invasion in 639 with a small army of some 4,000 men (later reinforced). With what seems astonishing speed, the Byzantine forces were routed and had withdrawn from Egypt by 642. An attempt by a Byzantine fleet and army to reconquer Alexandria in 645 was quickly defeated by the Arabs.

Various explanations have been given for the speed with which the conquest was achieved, most of which stress the weakness of Byzantine resistance rather than Arab strength. Certainly the division of the Byzantine government and army into autonomous provincial units militated against the possibility of a concerted and coordinated response. Although there is only dubious evidence for the claim that the Copts welcomed the Arab invasion in the belief that Muslim religious tolerance would be preferable to Byzantine enforced orthodoxy and repression, Coptic support for their Byzantine oppressors was probably unenthusiastic at best.

Early Arab Rule

In Egypt—as in Syria, Iraq, and Iran—the Arab conquerors did little in the beginning to disturb the status quo; as a small religious and ethnic minority, they thus hoped to make the occupation permanent. Treaties concluded between ʿAmr and the *muqawqis* (presumably a title referring to Cyrus, archbishop of Alexandria) granted protection to the native population in exchange for the payment of tribute. There was no attempt to force, or even to persuade, the Egyptians to convert to Islam; the Arabs even pledged to preserve the Christian churches. The Byzantine system of taxation, combining a tax on land with a poll tax, was maintained, though it was streamlined and centralized for the sake of efficiency. The tax was administered by Copts, who staffed the tax bureau at all but the highest levels.

To the mass of inhabitants, the conquest must have made little practical difference, because the Muslim rulers, in the beginning at least, left them alone as long as they paid their taxes; if anything, their lot may have been slightly easier, because Byzantine religious persecution had ended. Moreover, the Arabs deliberately isolated themselves from the native population, according to 'Umar's decree that no Arab could own land outside the Arabian Peninsula; this policy aimed at preventing the Arab tribal armies from dispersing and at ensuring a steady revenue from agriculture, on the assumption that the former landowners would make better farmers than would the Arab nomads.

As was their policy elsewhere, the conquerors refrained from using an established city such as Alexandria as their capital; instead, they founded a new garrison town (Arabic: *miṣr*), laid out in tribal quarters. As the site for this town they chose the strategic apex of the triangle formed by the Nile delta—at that time occupied by the Byzantine fortified township of Babylon. They named the town Al-Fusṭāṭ, which is probably an Arabized form of the Greek term for "encampment" and gives a good indication of the nature of the earliest settlement. Like garrison towns founded by the Arabs in Iraq—Al-Baṣrah and Al-Kūfah—Al-Fusṭāṭ became the main agency of Arabization in Egypt, inasmuch as it was the only town with an Arab majority and therefore required an extensive knowledge of Arabic from the native inhabitants.

The process of Arabization, however, was gradual. Arabic did not displace Greek as the official language of state until 706, and there is evidence that Coptic continued to be used as a spoken language in Al-Fusṭāṭ. Given the lack of pressure from the conquerors, the spread of their religion must have been even slower than that of their language. A mosque was built in Al-Fusṭāṭ bearing the name of ʿAmr ibn al-ʿĀṣ, and each quarter of the town had its own smaller mosque. ʿAmr's mosque served not only as the religious centre of the town but also as the seat of certain administrative and judicial activities.

Although Alexandria was maintained as a port city, Al-Fusṭāṭ, built on the Nile bank, was itself an important port and remained so until the 14th century. ʿAmr enhanced the port's commercial significance by clearing and reopening Trajan's Canal, so that shipments of grain destined for Arabia could be sent from Al-Fusṭāṭ to the Red Sea by ship rather than by caravan.

Egypt Under the Caliphate

For more than 200 years—that is, throughout the Umayyad caliphate and well into the ʿAbbāsid—Egypt was ruled by governors appointed by the caliphs. As a province in an empire, Egypt's status was much the same as it had been for centuries under foreign rulers whose main interest was to supply the central government with Egyptian taxes and grain. In spite of evidence that the Arab governors tried in general to collect the taxes equitably, taking into account the capacities of individual landowners to pay and the annual variations in agricultural yield, resistance to paying the taxes increased in the 8th century and sometimes erupted into rebellion in times of economic distress. Periodically, religious unrest was manifested in the form of political insurrections, especially in those exceptional times when a governor openly discriminated against the Copts by forcing them to wear distinctive clothing or, worse, by destroying their icons. Still, the official policy, especially in Umayyad times, was tolerance, partly for fiscal reasons. In order to maintain the higher tax revenues collected from non-Muslims, the Arab governors discouraged conversion to Islam and even required those who did convert to continue paying the non-Muslim tax. New Christian churches were sometimes built, and the government took an interest in the selection of patriarchs.

More than just a source of grain and taxes, Egypt also became a base for Arab-Muslim expansion by both land and sea. The former Byzantine shipyards in Alexandria provided the nucleus of an Egyptian navy, which between 649 and 669 joined in expeditions with Muslim fleets from Syria against the islands of Rhodes, Cyprus, and Sicily and defeated the Byzantine navy in a major battle at Phoenix (present-day Finike, Tur.) in 655. By land, the Arab armies advanced both to the south and to the west. As early as 651–652 the governor of Egypt invaded Nubia and imposed a treaty that required the Nubians to pay an annual tribute and to permit the unmolested practice of Islam in the province. Raids against North Africa by Arab armies based in Egypt began in 647; by 670 the Arabs had succeeded in establishing a garrison city in Ifrīqiyyah (now Tunisia), called Kairouan (Al-Qayrawān), which thenceforth displaced Egypt as the base for further expansion.

While some Arabs were passing through Egypt on their way to campaign in North Africa, others were being sent to the Nile valley on a permanent basis. In addition to tribal contingents that at times escorted newly appointed governors to Egypt (some of which settled in towns), tribesmen were sometimes imported and settled in an effort to increase the Arab-Muslim concentration in the vicinity of Al-Fusṭāṭ. The settlement of large numbers of anarchic tribesmen in Egypt, with tribal ties and allegiances elsewhere in the empire, meant that Egypt often became embroiled in political difficulties with the central government. Civil strife centring on the assassination of the caliph ʿUthmān ibn ʿAffān in 656 began in Egypt, where the tribesmen resented the favouritism shown by the caliph to members of his own family. Uprisings led by the dissident Khārijite sect were frequent in the mid-8th century. In the 9th century the ʿAbbāsid caliph al-Ma'mun (ruled 813–833) himself led an army from Iraq to put down a rebellion raised both by tribesmen and by Copts; repression of the Copts accompanying their defeat in 829–830 is usually cited as an important factor in accelerating conversion to Islam.

The difficulty inherent in ruling Egypt from Baghdad, which was itself undergoing stress and turbulence, is evident from the rapid turnover in governors assigned to Egypt; al-Ma'mūn's father, the caliph Hārūn al-Rashīd (ruled 786–809), for example, appointed 24 governors in a reign of 23 years. In order to strengthen their armies, the ʿAbbāsid caliphs had begun early in the 9th century to form contingents of Turkish slaves known as *mamlūk*s ("owned men"). To finance these new military formations and, in particular, to pay the Turkish commanders who headed them, the caliphs began to give them administrative grants (*iqṭāʿ* in Arabic, usually translated, albeit inaccurately, "fief") consisting of tax revenues from certain territories.

Possibly as a means of both removing the governorship from the level of tribal strife and paying the central government's Turkish *mamlūk*s, the caliphs began assigning the administration of Egypt to Turks rather than to Arabs. But this policy resulted in no tangible improvement in the administration of Egyptian affairs until 868, when Egypt was granted as a fief to the Turkish general Babak, who chose to remain in Iraq but appointed his stepson, a young *mamlūk* named Aḥmad ibn Ṭūlūn, as his agent in Egypt. Aḥmad's great achievement was that he quickly established his own authority in Egypt and backed it up with an army of his own creation, powerful enough to defy the central government of Baghdad and to embark upon foreign expansion.

Though short-lived, the Ṭūlūnid dynasty succeeded in restoring a measure of Egypt's ancient glory and inaugurated a new phase of Egyptian history. For the first time since the pharaohs, Egypt became virtually autonomous and the bulk of its revenues remained within its borders. What is more, Egypt became the centre of a small empire when Aḥmad conquered Syria and Palestine in 878–879. These developments were paralleled in other provinces of the ʿAbbāsid empire and were the direct result of the decline of the caliph's power.

The Ṭūlūnid Dynasty (868–905)

Aḥmad's first step upon his arrival in Egypt was to eliminate possible rivals. From an early date the administration of Egypt had been divided between the *amīr* (military governor), appointed by the caliph, and the *ʿāmil* (fiscal officer), who was sometimes appointed by the caliph, sometimes by the governor. When Aḥmad entered Egypt in 868 he found the office of *ʿāmil* filled by one Ibn al-Mudabbir, who over a period of years had gained control of Egyptian finances, enriching himself in the process, and was therefore reluctant to acknowledge Aḥmad's authority. A struggle for power soon broke out between the two, which ended four years later with the transfer of Ibn al-Mudabbir to Syria and the assumption of his duties and powers by Aḥmad. An even more important step for Aḥmad was the acquisition of an army that would be independent of the caliphate and loyal to him. To build such an army, Aḥmad resorted to the same method the caliphs themselves used—the purchase of *mamlūk*s, who could be trained as military units loyal to their owner.

In 877, when Aḥmad failed to pay Egypt's full contribution to the 'Abbāsid campaign during the Zanj rebellion in Iraq, the caliphal government, dominated by the caliph's brother al-Muwaffaq, realized that Egypt was slipping from imperial control. An expedition dispatched by al-Muwaffaq to remove Aḥmad from the governorship failed. Taking advantage of the caliphate's preoccupation with the revolt, Aḥmad in 878 invaded Palestine and Syria, where he occupied the principal cities and garrisoned them with his troops. Thereafter he signified his autonomy by imprinting his name on the coinage along with that of the caliph. Although the regent al-Muwaffaq lacked the resources to engage Aḥmad in battle, he did have him publicly cursed in the mosques of the empire as a means of retaliation.

Internally, Aḥmad took active measures to raise Egyptian agricultural productivity and thereby to increase tax revenues; the huge surplus he left in the state treasury at his death in 884 is a measure of his success. Another tangible indication of his achievement for Egypt is the enormous mosque bearing his name, erected in a suburb of Al-Fusṭāṭ, which is now Cairo; in contrast, no building comparable in grandeur had even been contemplated by the governors who preceded him.

The great benefits Aḥmad had gained for Egypt by keeping its resources within the country were squandered by his son and successor, Khumārawayh. He expended huge sums on luxurious appointments for his residence and paid a fortune as a dowry for a daughter he married to the caliph al-Mu'taḍid (ruled 892–902) in 895. Nevertheless, Khumārawayh was able to maintain the Egyptian armies in the field, and he led them to victory both in Syria and in Mesopotamia. He resolved his father's conflict with the caliphate by a combination of arms and diplomacy, so that Khumārawayh's authority over Egypt, Syria, and

Aḥmad ibn Ṭūlūn

(b. September 835—d. March 884, Egypt)

Aḥmad ibn Ṭūlūn was the eponymous founder of the Ṭūlūnid dynasty in Egypt and the first Muslim governor of Egypt to annex Syria.

As a child Aḥmad was taken into slavery and placed in the private service of the ʿAbbāsid caliph at Baghdad. Later he studied theology in the city of Tarsus (now in Turkey). He rose in the administrative structure of the ʿAbbāsid government and in 868 became a lieutenant in the service of the governor of Egypt. In Egypt he saw that the real centre of authority lay with the minister of finance, and during the next years he struggled to bring that department under his control. He was

Arcade and courtyard of the Mosque of Aḥmad ibn Ṭūlūn, Cairo. Bright/M. Grimoldi

successful, and he became vice-governor. Using a rebellion in Palestine as a pretext, he purchased a large number of slaves to increase the strength of his army, which formed the basis of his personal authority. In 882, using the excuse of a holy war against the Byzantine Empire, he annexed Syria. Aḥmad never went so far as to declare formal independence from the ʿAbbāsid caliph, but the autonomy of his rule was clearly a threat to the caliphal authority, and he ceased to send any tribute to the ʿAbbāsid government. The caliph himself was preoccupied with other problems and was unable to spare the military forces necessary to bring Aḥmad into submission.

Among Aḥmad's achievements was the significant prosperity generated by his economic policies in Egypt. By increasing agricultural output, he was able to compound tax revenues, the success of which was attested to by the treasury surplus that remained upon his death. He is remembered also for the fine mosque that bears his name, which he constructed at his capital at Al-Qaṭāʾiʿ, situated to the north of Al-Fusṭāṭ (modern Cairo).

Mesopotamia was given official caliphal recognition. This apparent strength evaporated when Khumārawayh was murdered in 896, leaving no funds with which his 14-year-old heir could pay the troops. The entire country fell into anarchy, which lasted until 905 when a caliphal army invaded Egypt and momentarily restored it to the status of a province ruled by governors sent from Baghdad.

The Ikhshīdid Dynasty (935–969)

For 30 years the governors were unable to restore stability in Egypt. During this time, Egypt was subjected to attacks from the Shīʿite Fāṭimid dynasty based in North Africa and to the rampages of an unruly domestic army. The appointment of Muḥammad ibn Ṭughj, from Sogdiana in Central Asia, as governor in 935 led to a repetition of Aḥmad's achievement; by bold measures Muḥammad established his authority over the treasury and the army, reasserted Egyptian influence in Syria, thwarted the Fāṭimids, and won the governorship of the holy cities of Arabia (Mecca and Medina). In addition, he founded a dynasty; his sons inherited his Sogdian princely title of *ikhshīd*, but their authority was usurped by their Abyssinian (Ethiopian) slave tutor, Abū al-Misk Kāfūr, who eventually ruled Egypt with the caliph's sanction. When Kāfūr died in 968 the Ikhshīdids were unable to maintain order in the army and the bureaucracy. In the following year the Fāṭimids took advantage of the disorder in Egypt to launch yet another attack, this one so successful that it led to the occupation of the country by an Amazigh (Berber) army led by the Fāṭimid general Jawhar.

The Fāṭimid Dynasty (969–1171)

The transfer of the Fāṭimid caliphate in 973 to the newly built palace city of Cairo had dramatic consequences for the evolution of Islamic Egypt. Politically, the Fāṭimids went a step further than the Ṭūlūnids by setting up Egypt as an independent rival to the ʿAbbāsid caliphate. In fact, an avowed aim of the early Fāṭimid propagandists (Arabic: *duʿāh*, singular *dāʿī*) was to achieve world dominion, eradicating the ʿAbbāsid caliphate in the process. For a variety of reasons they achieved neither of these goals; nevertheless, at the height of Fāṭimid power at the beginning of the 11th century, the Fāṭimid caliph could claim sovereignty over the whole of coastal North Africa, Sicily, the Hejaz and Yemen in Arabia, and southern Syria and Palestine. Although actual political-military control was never firm except in Egypt, allegiance paid to the Fāṭimids by their provinces was just as meaningful as that paid to the ʿAbbāsids and for a time was certainly more widespread.

Even when the Fāṭimid state fell into decline later in the 11th century and abandoned its imperial vision, Egypt continued to play an independent role in the Islamic world under the leadership of Armenian generals who had gained control of the Fāṭimid armies.

Islamization

It is difficult to estimate the religious change effected by the new dynasty except on the level of the governmental elite, which espoused the official doctrine of Ismāʿīlī Shīʿism—the branch that held all authority in the line of Ismāʿīl, who had predeceased his father, the sixth ʿAlid imam Jaʿfar ibn Muḥammad. Because they believed that the Fāṭimid caliph was the only legitimate leader, the practice of Sunni Islam was theoretically outlawed in Fāṭimid domains. But the practical difficulties which the Ismāʿīlī minority faced in imposing its will on the Sunni majority meant that the Muslim population of Egypt remained predominantly Sunni throughout the Fāṭimid period. Certainly there was no public outcry when Saladin, who founded the Ayyūbid dynasty, restored Egypt to Sunni rule in 1171. Regarding non-Muslims, the Fāṭimids, with one notable exception, were known for their tolerance, and the Copts continued to serve in the bureaucracy. Several Copts held the highest administrative post—the vizierate—without changing their religion. Jews also figured prominently in the government; in fact, a Jewish convert to Islam, Ibn Killis, was the first Fāṭimid vizier and is credited with laying the foundations of the Fāṭimid administrative system, in which the viziers exercised great power. Christians and Jews even managed to survive the reign of the so-called mad caliph, al-Ḥākim (ruled 996–1021), who ordered the destruction of Christian churches in Fāṭimid territory, including the Church of the Holy

Sepulchre in Jerusalem, and offered his non-Muslim subjects the choice of conversion to Islam or expulsion from Fāṭimid territory. This period of persecution undoubtedly accelerated the rate of conversion to Islam, if only on a temporary and superficial level.

In comparison with Iraq, Egypt contributed relatively little to Arabic literature and Islamic learning during the early ʿAbbāsid period. But the Fāṭimids' intense interest in propagating Ismāʿīlī Shīʿism through a network of missionary propagandists made Egypt an important religious and intellectual centre. The founding of the mosque-college of al-Azhar as well as of other academies drew Shīʿite scholars to Egypt from all over the Muslim world and stimulated the production of original contributions in literature, philosophy, and the Islamic sciences.

Arabization

The Arabization of Egypt continued at a slow pace. The early Fāṭimids' reliance on Amazigh troops was soon balanced by the importation of Turkish, Sudanese, and Arab contingents. The Fāṭimids are said to have used thousands of nomadic Arabs in the Egyptian cavalry and to have further stimulated Arabization by settling large numbers of Arabian tribesmen in Upper Egypt to deprive the Qarmaṭians—their Ismāʿīlī rivals in Iraq and Arabia—of Arab tribal support. On the other hand, the Fāṭimids reduced the Arab population of Egypt in the mid-11th century when they incited the Banū Hilāl and the Banū Ṣulaym tribes to emigrate from Egypt into the neighbouring Amazigh kingdom of Ifrīqiyyah.

Growth of Trade

One of the most far-reaching changes in Fāṭimid times was the growth of Egyptian commerce, especially in Al-Fusṭāṭ, which had become the port city for Cairo, the Fāṭimid capital. Theretofore, Iraq in the east and Tunisia in the west had been flourishing centres for trade conducted both within the Muslim world and between the Muslim and the Christian empires of the West. A number of factors contributed to alter this situation in favour of Egypt. As centralized power declined in Iraq, Mesopotamia, and Syria during the 9th and 10th centuries, traffic on the trade routes across these areas also declined. In Egypt, however, the establishment of a strong government, which soon controlled the Red Sea and maintained a strong navy in the eastern Mediterranean, offered an attractive alternative for the international transit trade between the Eastern and Western worlds. In addition to having the political stability essential for trade, the Fāṭimids encouraged commerce by their low tariff policy and their noninterference in the affairs of merchants who did business in Egypt. These factors, along with increased European mercantile activity in the Italian cities, helped restore Egypt as a great international entrepôt.

The End of the Fāṭimid Dynasty

The Fāṭimid achievement in restoring to Egypt a measure of its ancient glory was remarkable but brief. Halfway through their history the political-religious authority of the Fāṭimid caliphs was vitiated by military uprisings that could be put down only by force. By 1163 the Fāṭimid caliph had been shunted aside in a power struggle between the vizier and the chamberlain, who were themselves so impotent that they had to seek help from the Sunni and even from the Crusader powers of Syria and Palestine. Thus began a series of invasions at the behest of Fāṭimid officials, which ended in 1169 with the occupation of Egypt by an army from Syria, one of whose commanders—Saladin—was appointed Fāṭimid vizier. Two years later Saladin restored Egypt to ʿAbbāsid allegiance, abolished the Fāṭimid caliphate, and, in effect, established the Ayyūbid dynasty.

The Ayyūbid Dynasty (1171–1250)

Under Saladin and his descendants, Egypt was reintegrated into the Sunni world of the eastern caliphate. Indeed, during the period of the Crusades, Egypt became champion of that world against the Crusaders and, as such, chief target of the Crusader armies. But this was a gradual process that required Saladin first to build an army strong enough to establish his power in Egypt and then to unite the factions of Syria and Mesopotamia under his leadership against the Europeans. By so doing he reconstituted the Egyptian empire, which included, in addition to the areas just named, Yemen, the Hejaz, and, with his victory at Ḥaṭṭīn and subsequent capture of Jerusalem (1187), a major part of the Holy Land.

The abolition of the Fāṭimid caliphate and the official reinstitution of Sunni Islam seems to have caused little perturbation in Egypt except for an uprising by the Fāṭimid palace guard, quickly suppressed. This undoubtedly meant that Ismāʿīlī Shīʿism was confined to Fāṭimid ruling circles.

Saladin's Policies

Saladin's remission of all taxes not explicitly sanctioned by Islamic law must have contributed to his own popularity as well as to the stability of his regime. To ensure the defense of his state against both internal and external enemies, he strengthened the fortifications of Cairo by building a citadel and extending the Fāṭimid city walls. In spite of the major military and propagandistic efforts he mounted against the Crusaders, Saladin continued to

The citadel of Saladin, Cairo. Katherine Young/EB Inc.

treat the Christians of Egypt with tolerance; the Coptic Church thrived under the Ayyūbids, and Copts still served the government. Saladin also treated the Christians of Jerusalem with magnanimity after the conquest of that city. Under Saladin the Jewish community enjoyed protection, and such noted scholars as Moses Maimonides—who was the sultan's personal physician—settled there.

Much to the consternation of the popes, trade between Egypt and the Italian city-states remained brisk, and the Egyptians were able to use raw materials provided by the Italian merchants to forge weapons against the Crusaders. The administration of Egypt stayed in the hands of the vast, mainly civilian, bureaucracy but was supervised by military officials.

Power Struggles

The Ayyūbids introduced a significant change in the governance of their empire that was decisive for the history of their rule in Egypt. Though the Ayyūbids were themselves of Kurdish descent, Saladin followed the Turkish practice of assigning the provinces as fiefdoms to members of his family. In theory, such a measure would ensure the loyalty of the provinces to the central government of Egypt through the loyalty of Ayyūbid kinsmen to their family leader. In practice, however, the measure led to recurrent power struggles in which each governor used his province as a base from which to defy the supreme Ayyūbid power of Egypt. The sultans al-Malik al-ʿĀdil (ruled 1207–18) and al-Malik al-Kāmil (ruled 1218–38) each succeeded in reuniting Syria and Egypt under his own leadership. Kāmil, especially, was able to exploit Frankish attacks—in the form of the Fifth Crusade, directed against Damietta—to rally family and provincial support for the defense of Egypt. Nevertheless, given the dissension within the Ayyūbid empire, it was clearly in the interest of the Egyptian sultan to reach a peaceful settlement with the Crusaders; this was achieved in 1229 by a truce between Kāmil and the Holy Roman emperor Frederick II. The agreement stipulated that Kāmil exchange possession of Jerusalem and other territory in the Holy Land for Frederick's guarantee to support the sultan against aggression from any source.

Growth of Mamlūk Armies

The only real security for Ayyūbid Egypt lay in its independent military strength. This explains why one of the last sultans, al-Ṣāliḥ Ayyūb (ruled 1240, 1245–49), resorted to increased purchase of Turkish *mamlūk*s as a means of manning his armies. Although slave troops had formed an important part of Egyptian armies since the time of Aḥmad ibn Ṭūlūn, their strength had been checked by racial dissension among the various slave units as well as the presence of nonslave elements. But after the death of al-Ṣālih Ayyūb in the course of the Crusade of Louis IX—which *mamlūk* troops were crucial in thwarting—a group of rebellious *mamlūk*s assassinated his son and successor Tūrān-Shah and elevated al-Ṣālih's wife Shajar al-Durr to the throne in 1250. Her brief rule marked the first time a woman had ruled Egypt since Roman times, but, pressured by the rebellious Ayyūbid emirs in Syria and by the ʿAbbāsid caliph in Baghdad (all of whom demanded that a man rule Egypt), she married a *mamlūk* general named Aybak. The assassination in 1257 of both queen and consort occurred barely a year before Mongol armies stormed Baghdad and put an end to the ʿAbbāsid caliphate, leaving military slaves to rule Egypt with no legitimizing authority. High ranking *mamlūk*s had played a role in politics in the Islamic world since the 9th century; some had even seized political control (as in the Ghaznavid dynasty of Turkey). But for the first time a system arose—in what otherwise might have been a dynastic lapse—wherein former slaves stood at the head of a self-perpetuating slave dynasty. This new order, which came at a time when the light of Baghdad had been extinguished and which lasted for two and a half centuries, brought Egypt to a new cultural and political flowering.

THE MAMLŪK AND OTTOMAN PERIODS (1250–1800)

Egypt thrived under the Mamlūks from 1250 until their defeat by the Ottomans in 1517. Under Mamlūk rule, Egypt became one of the intellectual and cultural centres of the Arab and Islamic world, and after Mongol armies sacked Baghdad and ended the ʿAbbāsid caliphate in the mid-13th century, the Mamlūks established a pseudo-caliphate of dubious legitimacy. But in 1517 the Ottoman Empire defeated the Mamlūks and established control over Egypt that lasted until 1798, when Napoleon led a French army in a short occupation of the country.

The Mamlūk Rulers (1250–1517)

During the Mamlūk period Egypt became the unrivaled political, economic, and cultural centre of the eastern Arabic-speaking zone of the Muslim world. Symbolic of this development was the reestablishment in 1261 under the Mamlūk rulers of the ʿAbbāsid caliphate—destroyed by the Mongols in their sack of Baghdad three years earlier—with the arrival in Cairo of a youth claiming ʿAbbāsid lineage. Although the caliph enjoyed little authority, had no power, and was of dubious authenticity, the mere fact that the Mamlūks chose to maintain the institution in Cairo is a measure of their determination to dominate the Arab-Islamic world and to legitimize their own rule. It is curious that the Mamlūks—all of whom were of non-Arab (most were Turks and, later, Circassians), non-Muslim origin and some of whom knew little if any Arabic—founded a regime that established Egypt's supremacy in Arab culture.

Mamlūk legitimacy also rested on the regime's early military successes, particularly those against the Mongols, who were seen by many contemporaries as invincible and as a threat to the very existence of Islam as a political culture. In 1260, two years after the demoralizing sack of Baghdad, the Mongol leader sent an ambassador to Egypt to deliver terms of surrender. The Mamlūk leader, Quṭuz, who had come to power after the death of Aybak and Shajar al-Durr, ordered the Mongol ambassador put to death, thus insuring war against what seemed an unbeatable adversary. After their victory at the Battle of 'Ayn Jālūt later that year, however, the Mamlūks were able to roll back the Mongol armies from the Levant. This victory, and the success of subsequent Mamlūk sultans against the Crusaders in Syria and Palestine, lent a certain sanction to Mamlūk rule that it may otherwise never have attained.

Political Life

The political history of the Mamlūk state is complex; during their 264-year reign, no fewer than 45 Mamlūks gained the sultanate, and once, in desperate circumstances, a caliph (in 1412) was briefly installed as sultan. At times individual Mamlūks succeeded in establishing dynasties, most notably Sultan Qalā'ūn (ruled 1279–90), whose progeny ruled Egypt, with two short interruptions, until 1382. Often the Mamlūks chose to allow a sultan's son to succeed his father only for as long as it took another Mamlūk to build up enough support to seize the throne for himself. In reality there was no principle of legitimacy other than force, for without sufficient military power a sultan

Qalā'ūn

(d. 1290)

Al-Manṣūr Sayf al-Dīn Qalā'ūn al-Alfī, known as Qalā'ūn, was a Mamlūk sultan of Egypt (1279–90) and the founder of a dynasty that ruled for a century.

In the 1250s Qalā'ūn was an early and devoted supporter of the Mamlūk commander Baybars, and, after the latter became sultan of Egypt and Syria in 1260, Qalā'ūn's career advanced rapidly. Upon the death of Baybars in 1277, Qalā'ūn quickly deposed and exiled two of Baybars's sons who had briefly succeeded to the sultanate, and in 1279 Qalā'ūn himself became sultan of Egypt. He solidified his power after fighting off a rival claimant to the throne in 1280, and he thereupon proceeded to consolidate the Mamlūk position in the Middle East.

Qalā'ūn wished both to expel the Latin (Christian) Crusaders from their remaining footholds in the Middle East and to repel the invading Mongols. He made a truce with the Knights Templar and then ended the Mongol threat to Egypt by defeating the Mongols at Ḥomṣ in 1281. In 1289 he broke his truce with the Crusaders and captured the fortified port of Tripoli, which was then the largest town still held by the Crusaders. Qalā'ūn died while mounting a campaign to besiege the town of Acre (now 'Akko, Israel). He was succeeded as sultan by his son Khalīl, who successfully wrested Acre from the Crusaders in 1291. Qalā'ūn was a decisive ruler and an able administrator. He encouraged trade and public-welfare activities in Egypt and was responsible for building the Qalā'ūn Mosque complex that survives in Cairo.

could expect to be overthrown by a stronger Mamlūk. It was a period of raw political brutality seldom paralleled in world history.

Nevertheless, several sultans succeeded in harnessing the energies of the Mamlūk system to establish internal stability and to embark on foreign conquests. Soon after the Mamlūk victory over the Mongols at 'Ayn Jālūt in 1260,

Baybars I seized power by assassinating Quṭuz. He was the true founder of the Mamlūk state, and he campaigned actively and with success against the remaining Crusader possessions in Palestine and Syria. He ruled until 1277. During the long reign of al-Malik al-Nāṣir (ruled 1293–1341), the Mamlūks concluded a truce with the Mongols (1323) after several major battles and, in spite of widespread famine, outbreaks of religious strife, and Bedouin uprisings, maintained economic prosperity in Egypt and peaceful relations with foreign powers both Muslim and Christian.

Although the state began to decline politically and economically after the death of Nāṣir in 1341, Egypt continued to dominate the eastern Arab world. But the cumulative effect of the plague (which swept Egypt in 1348 and on many occasions subsequently), Timur's victory in Syria in 1400, and Egypt's loss to the Portuguese of control over the Indian trade, along with the sultans' inability to keep their refractory Mamlūk corps under control, gradually sapped the strength of the state. The best efforts of such a vigorous sultan as Qā'it Bāy (ruled 1468–96) failed to make Egypt strong enough to defend its Syrian provinces against raids by the Turkoman states of Anatolia and Azerbaijan and campaigns of the Ottoman Empire.

Contributions to Arabic Culture

By the time of the Mamlūks, the Arabization of Egypt must have been almost complete. Arabic had been the language of the bureaucracy since the early 8th century and the language of religion and culture even longer. Moreover, the prevalence of Arabic as a written and spoken language is attested by the discovery in the *genizah* (storeroom) of a Cairo synagogue of thousands of letters and documents—called the Genizah Documents—dating from the 11th through the 13th century. Though often written in Hebrew characters, the actual language of most of these documents is Arabic, which proves that Arabic was widely used even by non-Muslims. The main incentive for learning Arabic must have come from the desire of a subject population to learn the administrative and scholarly language of the ruling and learned elite. The immigration of Arab tribesmen during the early centuries of the occupation, and their intermarriage with the indigenous inhabitants, must also have contributed to the gradual spread of Arabic in Egypt.

The specific Mamlūk contribution to Arabic culture (i.e., the ethnically diverse community united by the Arabic language), however, lay above all in military achievement. By defeating the Mongols, the Mamlūks provided a haven in Syria and in Egypt for Muslims fleeing from Mongol devastation. The extent of this haven was narrowed by subsequent Mongol attacks against Syria, so that Egypt received an influx of refugees from Syria itself as well as from areas farther east.

This accidental displacement of scholars and artisans into Egypt does not, however, wholly account for the efflorescence of certain types of cultural activity under the Mamlūks. In the same way that they supported the caliphate as a visible symbol of their legitimate claim to rule Islamic territory, the Mamlūks cultivated and patronized religious leaders whose skills they needed in administering their empire and in directing the religious sentiments of the masses into safe (i.e., nondisruptive) channels. Those divines who cooperated with the state were rewarded with government offices in the case of the ulama (Arabic: *ʿulamāʾ*; religious scholars) and with endowed *zāwiyah*s (monasteries) in the case of the Sufis (mystics). On the other hand, those who dared criticize the prevailing social and moral order were thrown into prison; such was the fate of renowned legist Ibn Taymiyyah (1263–1328), who, having emigrated from Mesopotamia to escape the Mongols, was incarcerated in Cairo by the Mamlūks for spreading doctrines that their religious functionaries considered heresy.

Concrete evidence of the stimulus the Mamlūks gave to cultural life in an era of economic prosperity can be found chiefly in the fields of architecture and historiography. Dozens of public buildings erected under Mamlūk patronage are still standing in Cairo and include mosques, madrasahs, hospitals, *zāwiyah*s, and caravansaries. Historical writing under the Mamlūks was equally monumental, in the form of immense chronicles, biographical dictionaries, and encyclopaedias.

Religious Life

The Mamlūk period is also important in Egyptian religious history. With few and therefore notable exceptions, the Muslim rulers of Egypt had seldom interfered with the lives of their Christian and Jewish subjects so long as these groups paid the special taxes (known as *jizyah*) levied on them in exchange for state protection. Indeed, both Copts and Jews had always served in the Muslim bureaucracy, sometimes in the very highest administrative positions. Even the Crusades apparently failed to upset the delicate balance between Muslims and Christians. Trade with the Italian city-states had certainly continued, and there is no evidence that the local Christians were held accountable for the Crusader invasions of Egypt.

With the establishment of the Mamlūk sultanate, however, it is generally agreed that the lot of the Christians, both in Egypt and in Syria, took a distinct turn for the worse. One indication of this change is the increased production of anti-Christian polemics written by Muslim theologians. A possible reason for the change may have been the association of Christians with the Mongol peril. Because the Mongols used Christian auxiliaries in their armies—Georgians and Armenians in particular—they often spared the Christian populations of towns they conquered, while slaughtering the Muslims. Also, the diplomatic efforts aimed at uniting the Mongols with Christian European powers in a joint Crusade against the Muslims might have contributed to the Mamlūks' distrust of the Christians. But the dissatisfaction seems to have originated not so much with the Mamlūk rulers as with the masses, and it seems to have been directed not so much against Christians' sympathy for the Mongols as against their privileged position and role in the Mamlūk state.

On several occasions popular resentment against the Copts' conspicuous wealth and their employment in the government was manifested in public demonstrations. Both Muslims and Christians resorted to arson, burning the others' sanctuaries to express their hatred. Under such pressure, the Mamlūk government dismissed Christians from the bureaucracy on no fewer than nine occasions between 1279 and 1447. (It was, however, usually necessary to appoint new Copts, since they alone understood the accounting system that had been used since pharaonic times.) In 1301 the Mamlūks ordered all the churches in Egypt to be closed. As a result of these intermittent persecutions and the destruction of churches, it is believed that the rate of conversion to Islam accelerated markedly in the Mamlūk period and that Coptic virtually disappeared except as a liturgical language. By the end of Mamlūk rule, the Muslims may well have reached the same numerical superiority that they enjoy in modern times—a ratio of perhaps 10:1.

Economic Life

In trade and commerce, the Mamlūk period marks the zenith of medieval Egyptian economic history. During the 13th and 14th centuries (as long, that is, as the sultanate was able to maintain order in Egypt), trade was heavy with Mediterranean and Black sea ports and with India. The Oriental trade was controlled largely by a group of Muslim merchants known as the Kārimīs; the Mediterranean trade was left to European traders, whom the Mamlūks allowed certain privileges in Alexandria. By the 15th century, however, Egypt's commercial importance rapidly deteriorated as the result of population losses caused by the plague, increased government interference in commerce, Bedouin raiding, and Portuguese competition in the Indian trade.

The Ottomans (1517–1798)

With the Ottomans' defeat of the Mamlūks in 1516–17, Egyptian medieval history had come full circle, as Egypt reverted to the status of a province governed from Constantinople (present-day Istanbul). Again the country was exploited as a source of taxation for the benefit of an imperial government and as a base for foreign expansion. The economic decline that had begun under the late Mamlūks continued, and with it came a decline in Egyptian culture.

Some historians attribute the lethargy of Egypt in this era solely to the rule of Constantinople. But, although Ottoman policy was geared to imperial, not Egyptian, needs, it was obviously to the rulers' benefit to provide a stable government that would maintain Egyptian agriculture at a high level of productivity and would promote the transit trade. To a certain extent Ottoman actions served these purposes. The decisive factor that ultimately undermined Ottoman policies was the perpetuation of the former Mamlūk elite; though they collaborated with the Ottoman government, they often defied it and ultimately came to dominate it. By and large, the history of Ottoman Egypt concerns the process by which the conquered Mamlūks reasserted their power within the Egyptian state.

The Ottoman Conquest

From the conquest itself, the Ottoman presence in Egypt was entangled with Mamlūk factionalism. There is no doubt that the Ottomans invaded Syria in 1516 to thwart an incipient coalition against Ottoman expansion between the Ṣafavid dynasty of Persia and the Mamlūks of Egypt and Syria. The long-standing enmity between the Ottomans and the Mamlūks arose from their contest to control the Turkoman frontier states north of Syria. After the Ottomans strengthened their hold over eastern Anatolia in 1514, it was only natural that the Mamlūks should attempt to bolster their forces in northern Syria and exchange diplomatic missions with the Ṣafavids. The Ottoman sultan Selim I (the Grim) responded by attacking the reinforced Mamlūk army in Syria, probably as a preliminary step in a new campaign against the Ṣafavids. In 1516, after Selim had defeated the Mamlūks at Marj Dābiq (north of Aleppo), Ottoman goals had probably been met, especially since the Mamlūk sultan Qānṣūh al-Ghawrī died in the battle. But the Mamlūks rallied around a new sultan in Cairo who refused to accept Selim's terms for a settlement. Spurred on by the Mamlūk traitor Khayr Bey, Selim marched against Egypt in 1517, defeated the Mamlūks, and installed Khayr Bey as Ottoman governor. Khayr Bey died in 1522; thereafter, the Ottoman viceroy (called *vali*), with the title of pasha, was sent from Constantinople.

Ottoman Administration

In 1525 the Ottoman administration of Egypt was defined and codified by the Ottoman grand vizier, İbrahim Paşa,

Ottoman sultan Selim I. Hulton Archive/Getty Images

who was dispatched to Egypt for this purpose by the sultan Süleyman I (the Magnificent). According to the terms of İbrahim Paşa's decree (*kanun-name*), Egypt was to be ruled by a viceroy aided by an advisory council (divan) and an army comprising both Ottoman and local corps. The collection of taxes and the administration of the four provinces into which Egypt was divided were assigned to inspectors (*kashif*s). Although the Egyptian government was headed by bureaucratic officials sent from Constantinople, and supported by Ottoman troops, the Mamlūks were able to penetrate both the bureaucracy and the army. The *kashif*s were often drawn from Mamlūk ranks; three of the seven military corps formed by the Ottomans in the 16th century were recruited in Egypt, one of which—the Circassians—was composed of Circassian Mamlūks. Their service in the army enabled the Mamlūk emirs to secure high-ranking military posts that entitled them to serve on the divan itself.

By the 17th century a distinct elite bearing the title of bey had emerged, which consisted largely of Mamlūk emirs. These beys held no specific offices but were nevertheless paid a salary by the Ottoman government. The elite was perpetuated through the old Mamlūk system of purchasing slaves, giving them military training, then freeing them and attaching them to one of the great Mamlūk houses of Egypt. Thus, for all practical purposes, the Mamlūks maintained themselves as an elite throughout the Ottoman period. They were no longer the only political-military elite, as they had been in the past, but they ultimately succeeded in reestablishing their dominance. Yet the chief obstacle to the growth of their power was not so much the Ottoman ruling hierarchy as it was their own factionalism. During the 17th and 18th centuries, the Mamlūks were divided into two great rival houses—the Faqāriyyah and the Qāsimiyyah—whose mutual hostility often broke out into fighting and impaired the strength of the Mamlūks as a bloc.

Mamlūk Power Under the Ottomans

In spite of internal dissension and the resistance of the non-Mamlūk hierarchy, the Mamlūks had emerged by the early 18th century as the supreme power in Egyptian politics. While the beys continued to acknowledge the authority of the Ottoman viceroy and to send tribute to Constantinople, the strongest single figure in Egypt was the bey who held the newly coined title of *shaykh al-balad* ("chief of the city"), which signified that he was recognized by the other beys as their chief. The Mamlūks' rise to power was climaxed by the careers of two emirs—ʿAlī Bey and Abū Dhahab—both of whom secured from the Sublime Porte (Ottoman government) de facto recognition of their autonomy in Egypt (1769–75) and even undertook military campaigns in Syria and the Hejaz. The Ottomans attempted to end the Mamlūk domination by sending an army to Egypt in 1786. Although it was initially successful, this attempt failed and the troops were withdrawn a year later. A Mamlūk duumvirate (two-person ruling coalition) was reestablished consisting of Murād Bey and Ibrāhīm Bey and lasted until Napoleon invaded Egypt in 1798.

Expansion

During the 16th century, when their regime in Egypt was strongest, the Ottomans used Egypt as a base for expansion to the south. Like the Mamlūk rulers before them, they attempted to control the southern approaches to Egypt by instituting their authority in Nubia; this they achieved by annexing Nubia as far south as the Third Cataract of the Nile River. Elsewhere, they undertook to reassert Egyptian command of the Red Sea, which the

'Alī Bey

(b. 1728, Abkhasia, Caucasus [now Abkhaziya, Georgia]—d. May 8, 1773, near Ṣāliḥiyyah, Egypt)

'Alī Bey was a Mamlūk governor of Egypt under Ottoman suzerainty who attempted to throw off the Ottoman Turkish rule.

'Alī Bey was an enslaved Caucasian who was made a gift to Ibrāhīm Katkhudā, an emir who was the virtual ruler of Egypt. 'Alī earned the confidence of his master, who later freed him and advanced him to the rank of bey. 'Alī managed to strengthen his position by obtaining slaves and setting them in high positions. His power thus recognized, he was made *shaykh al-balad*. He was involved in much political maneuvering and finally succeeded in becoming the virtually independent ruler of Egypt. He gained control of Mecca and then invaded and seized Syria. Betrayed by his army commander, he fled to Syria in 1772. He was defeated and captured in an attempt to recover Egypt, and he died of the wounds he suffered in battle.

Portuguese had begun to contest during the early 16th century. Ottoman fleets and troops captured Yemen and Aden (1536–46) and thus dominated the lower Red Sea; in 1557 they strengthened this position by setting up a colony on the Abyssinian coast at Mitsiwa (now Massawa, Eritrea). In the 17th century these outposts began to lose their importance as Ottoman and Portuguese power started to decline and the Dutch took over the spice trade.

Culture

Given the political instability and economic decline that had prevailed in Egypt since late Mamlūk times, it is not surprising that the culture of Ottoman Egypt lacked vitality. Perhaps the most telling example of intellectual quiescence was the dramatic decline in the quantity of historical works produced in Egypt. As already noted, the Mamlūk period is renowned for the number and quality of its historians, partly because the emirs patronized court historians; by contrast, in almost three centuries of Ottoman rule, Egypt produced only one historian worthy of note, ʿAbd al-Raḥmān al-Jabartī in the late 18th to early 19th century, famous for his observations on the French occupation. The Ottomans also fell short of the Mamlūks' achievement in architecture; while there is no lack of public buildings erected under Ottoman patronage, even the best of these are imitations of the Byzantine basilica, which had been adopted as the model for mosques.

Religious Affairs

Like all previous Muslim governments, the Ottomans continued to employ Copts in the financial offices of the bureaucracy. The Ottomans allowed the caliphate, so assiduously preserved in its nominal form by the Mamlūks, to lapse. At first the caliph was installed in Constantinople by Selim I. Later the caliph—purportedly the last of the ʿAbbāsid line—returned to Egypt, where he died in the reign of Süleyman. The claim that the caliph had transferred his authority to the Ottoman sultan is generally considered an 18th-century invention.

FROM THE FRENCH TO THE BRITISH OCCUPATION (1798–1882)

The French occupation, which began in 1798 and ended in 1801, marked the first time a European power had conquered and occupied Egypt, and it set the stage for further European involvement. Egypt's strategic location has always made it a hub for trade routes between Africa, Europe, and Asia, but this natural advantage was enhanced in 1869 by the opening of the Suez Canal, connecting the Mediterranean Sea to the Red Sea. The concern of the European powers (namely France and Britain, which were major shareholders in the canal) to safeguard the canal for strategic and commercial reasons became one of the most important factors influencing the subsequent history of Egypt.

The French Occupation and its Consequences (1798–1805)

Although several projects for a French occupation of Egypt had been advanced in the 17th and 18th centuries, the purpose of the expedition that sailed under Napoleon I from Toulon in May 1798 was specifically connected with the war against Britain. Napoleon had discounted the feasibility of an invasion of England but hoped, by occupying Egypt, to damage British trade, threaten India, and obtain assets for bargaining in any future peace settlement. Meanwhile, as a colony under the benevolent and progressive administration of Revolutionary France, Egypt was to be regenerated and would regain its ancient prosperity. The military and naval forces were therefore accompanied by a commission of scholars and scientists to investigate and report the past and present condition of the country.

Eluding the British Mediterranean fleet under Horatio Nelson, the French landed at Abū Qīr (Aboukir) Bay on July 1 and took Alexandria the next day. In an Arabic proclamation, Napoleon assured the Egyptians that he came as a friend to Islam and the Ottoman sultan, to punish the usurping Mamlūks and to liberate the people. From Alexandria the French advanced on Cairo, defeating Murād Bey at Shubrākhīt (July 13), and again decisively at Imbābah, opposite Cairo in the Battle of the Pyramids on July 21. Murād fled to Upper Egypt, while his colleague,

Ibrāhīm Bey, together with the Ottoman viceroy, made his way to Syria.

After entering Cairo (July 25), Napoleon sought to conciliate the population, especially the religious leaders (ulama), by demonstrating his sympathy with Islam and by establishing councils (divans) as a means of consulting Egyptian opinion. The destruction of the French fleet at Abū Qīr by Nelson in the Battle of the Nile on August 1 virtually cut Napoleon's communications and made it necessary for him to consolidate his rule and to make the expeditionary force as self-sufficient as possible. The savants, organized in the Institut d'Égypte, played their part in this. Meanwhile, Egyptian resentment of alien rule, administrative innovations, and the growing fiscal burden of military occupation was exacerbated when the Ottoman sultan, Selim III (ruled 1789–1807), declared war on France on September 11. An unforeseen revolt in Cairo on October 21 was suppressed after an artillery bombardment that ended any hopes of cordial Franco-Egyptian coexistence.

Ottoman Syria, dominated by Aḥmad al-Jazzār, the governor of Acre, was the base from which French-occupied Egypt might most easily be threatened, and Napoleon resolved to deny it to his enemies. His invasion force crossed the frontier in February 1799 but failed to take Acre after a protracted siege (March 19–May 20), and Napoleon evacuated Syrian territory. A seaborne Ottoman invading force landed at Abū Qīr in July but failed to maintain its bridgehead. At this point Napoleon resolved to return to France, and he succeeded in slipping away, past the British fleet, on August 22.

His successor as general in chief, Jean-Baptiste Kléber, viewed the situation of the expeditionary force with pessimism and, like many of the soldiers, wished to return to the theatre of war in Europe. He therefore entered into negotiations with the Ottomans and by the Convention of Al-ʿArīsh (Jan. 24, 1800) agreed to evacuate Egypt. Sir Sydney Smith, the British naval commander in the eastern Mediterranean, sponsored the convention, but in this he had exceeded his powers and was instructed by his superior officer, Admiral Lord Keith, to require the French to surrender as prisoners of war. Although the Ottoman reoccupation was well under way, Kléber and the French determined on resistance and defeated the Turkish forces at the Battle of Heliopolis (March 20). A second revolt of Cairo, fomented by Ottoman fugitives, took about a month to suppress; but French authority had been restored when Kléber was assassinated by a Syrian Muslim, Sulaymān al-Ḥalabī, on June 14.

His successor, ʿAbd Allāh Jacques Menou, a French officer (and former nobleman) who had converted to Islam, was determined to maintain the occupation and administered at first a tolerably settled country, although he lacked the prestige of his two predecessors. In 1801 a threefold invasion of Egypt began. British troops were landed at Abū Qīr in March, while the Ottomans advanced from Syria. Shortly afterward, British Indian forces were landed at Quṣayr on the Red Sea coast. The French garrison in Cairo capitulated in June and Menou himself at Alexandria in September.

The brief episode of the French occupation was to be significant for Egypt in several ways. The arrival of a European army accompanied by scholars and scientists appropriately inaugurated the impact of the West, which was to be felt increasingly afterward. Egypt, insulated for centuries by the Mamlūk and Ottoman sultanates, was no longer immune from European influence; it had become an object of the contending policies of France and Britain, a part of the Eastern Question. Napoleon's savants had little success in interpreting Western culture to the traditionalist ulama of Cairo; their achievement was rather to unveil Egypt to Europe. They uncovered the celebrated Rosetta Stone, which held a trilingual inscription making it possible to decipher hieroglyphs and which thus laid the foundation of modern Egyptology. Their reports and monographs were collected in the monumental *Description de l'Égypte* ("Description of Egypt"), which was published in parts from 1809 to 1828 in Paris.

Of more immediate consequence for Egypt was the effect of the French occupation on internal politics. The Mamlūk ascendancy was fatally weakened. Murād Bey, who had made his peace with the French, died shortly before their capitulation in 1801; and Ibrāhīm Bey, who returned to Egypt with the Ottomans, had henceforward little power. The new Mamlūk leaders, 'Uthmān Bey al-Bardīsī (died 1806) and Muḥammad Bey al-Alfī (died 1807), former retainers of Murād, headed rival factions and had in any case to reckon with the British and Ottoman occupation forces. In March 1803 the British troops were evacuated in accordance with the Treaty of Amiens (March 27, 1802). But the Ottomans, determined to reassert their control over Egypt, remained, establishing their power through a viceroy and an occupying army, in which the most effective fighting force was an Albanian contingent. The Albanians, however, acted as an independent party and in May 1803 mutinied and installed their leader as acting viceroy. When he was assassinated shortly afterward, the command of the Albanians passed to his lieutenant, Muḥammad 'Alī (ruled 1805–48), who, during the ensuing two years, cautiously strengthened his own position at the expense of both the Mamlūks and the Ottomans.

Battle of the Nile

The Battle of the Nile (also called the Battle of Aboukir [or Abukir] Bay) was one of the greatest victories of the British admiral Horatio Nelson. It was fought on Aug. 1, 1798, between the British and French fleets in Abū Qīr Bay, near Alexandria, Egypt.

In 1798 Napoleon Bonaparte made plans for an invasion of Egypt in order to constrict Britain's trade routes and threaten its possession of India. The British government heard that a large French naval expedition was to sail from a French Mediterranean port under the command of Napoleon, and in response it ordered the Earl of St. Vincent, the commander in chief of the British fleet, to detach ships under Rear Admiral Sir Horatio Nelson to reconnoitre off Toulon and to watch French naval movements there. But Nelson's own ship was dismasted in a storm, and his group of frigates, now dispersed, returned to the British base at Gibraltar. Meanwhile, St. Vincent

The all-night Battle of the Nile, fought on Aug. 1, 1798 between French Revolutionary forces and the British fleet under Horatio Nelson near Alexandria, Egypt, was a decisive victory for the British, securing their control of the Mediterranean. Edward Gooch/Hulton Archive/Getty Images

sent Nelson more ships, which joined Nelson on June 7, bringing his strength up to 14 ships of the line.

The French expedition eluded the British warships and sailed first for Malta, which the French seized from the British early in June. After spending a week at Malta, Napoleon sailed with his fleet for his main objective, Egypt. Meanwhile, Nelson had found Toulon empty and had correctly guessed the French objective, but because he lacked frigates for reconnaissance, he missed the French fleet, reached Egypt first, found the port of Alexandria empty, and impetuously returned to Sicily, where his ships were resupplied. Determined to find the French fleet, he sailed to Egypt once more and on August 1 he sighted the main French fleet of 13 ships of the line and 4 frigates under Admiral François-Paul Brueys d'Aigailliers at anchor in Abū Qīr Bay.

Although there were but a few hours left until nightfall and Brueys's ships were in a strong defensive position, being securely ranged in a sandy bay that was flanked on one side by a shore battery on Abū Qīr Island, Nelson gave orders to attack at once. Several of the British warships were able to maneuver around the head of the French line of battle and thus got inside and behind their position. Fierce fighting ensued, during which Nelson himself was wounded in the head. The climax came at about 10:00 pm, when Brueys's 120-gun flagship, which was by far the largest ship in the bay, blew up with most of the ship's company, including the admiral. The fighting continued for the rest of the night, with the end result that the British warships destroyed or captured all but two of Brueys's ships of the line. The British suffered about 900 casualties, the French about 10 times as many.

The Battle of the Nile had several important effects. It isolated Napoleon's army in Egypt, thus ensuring its ultimate disintegration. It ensured that in due time Malta would be retaken from the French, and it both heightened British prestige and secured British control of the Mediterranean.

Muḥammad ʿAlī and His Successors (1805–82)

In May 1805 a revolt broke out in Cairo against the Ottoman viceroy, Khūrshīd Pasha, after which the ulama invested Muḥammad ʿAlī as viceroy. For some weeks there

Muḥammad ʿAlī. Courtesy of the trustees of the British Museum; photograph, J.R. Freeman and Co. Ltd.

was street fighting, and Khūrshīd was besieged in the citadel. In July Sultan Selim III confirmed Muḥammad ʿAlī in office and the revolt ended.

Muḥammad ʿAlī's viceroyalty was marked by a series of military successes, some of which were attended by political failures that frustrated his wider aims. After the renewal of war between Britain and Napoleonic France in 1803, Egypt again became an area of strategic significance. A British expedition occupied Alexandria in 1807 but failed to capture Rosetta and, after a defeat at the hands of Muḥammad ʿAlī's forces, was allowed to withdraw.

MILITARY EXPANSION

In Arabia, the domination by puritanical Wahhābī Muslims of Islam's holy cities, Mecca and Medina, was a serious embarrassment to the Ottoman sultan, who was the titular overlord of the Arabian territory of the Hejaz and the leading Muslim sovereign. At the invitation of Sultan Mahmud II (ruled 1808–39), Muḥammad ʿAlī sent an expedition to Arabia that between 1811 and 1813 expelled the Wahhābīs from the Hejaz. In a further campaign (1816–18), Ibrāhīm Pasha, the viceroy's eldest son, defeated the Wahhābīs in their homeland of Najd and brought central Arabia within Egyptian control. In 1820–21 Muḥammad

'Alī sent an expedition up the Nile River and conquered much of what is now the northern portion of Sudan. By so doing, he made himself master of one of the principal channels of the slave trade and began an African empire that was to be expanded under his successors.

After the outbreak of the Greek insurrection against Ottoman rule, Muḥammad 'Alī, at Mahmud's request, suppressed the Cretan revolt in 1822. In 1825 Ibrāhīm began a victorious campaign in the Morea in southern Greece, where his military success provoked intervention by the European powers and brought on the destruction of the Ottoman and Egyptian fleets at the Battle of Navarino (Oct. 20, 1827). The Morea was evacuated the following year.

In 1831 Muḥammad 'Alī embarked upon the invasion of Syria. His pretext was a quarrel with the governor of Acre, but deeper considerations were involved, particularly the growing strength of the sultan, which might threaten his own autonomy. Syria, moreover, was strategically important; and its products, especially timber, usefully complemented the Egyptian economy. The viceroy's forces defeated the Ottomans at Kütahya near Konya in Anatolia (December 1832), and in 1833 the sultan ceded his Syrian provinces to Muḥammad 'Alī.

In 1839 Ottoman forces reentered Syria but were defeated by Ibrāhīm at the Battle of Nizip (June 24). A fortnight later Mahmud II died, and the Ottoman Empire, seemingly on the verge of dissolution, was saved only by European intervention. In 1840 the European powers compelled Ibrāhīm to evacuate Syria. Muḥammad 'Alī's Arabian empire (which since 1833 had extended into Yemen) crumbled at the same time. Although in 1841 the new sultan, Abdülmecid I (ruled 1839–61), conferred on the family of Muḥammad 'Alī the hereditary rule of Egypt, the viceroy's powers were declining. Because of the viceroy's growing senility, Ibrāhīm took power in July 1848. But the son's reign lasted only a few months until his death the following November. The next viceroy was ʿAbbās I (ruled 1848–54), the eldest grandson of Muḥammad ʿAlī (who died in 1849).

ADMINISTRATIVE CHANGES

Muḥammad ʿAlī's military exploits would not have been possible but for radical changes within the administration of Egypt itself. Muḥammad ʿAlī was a pragmatic statesman whose principal objective was to secure for himself and his family the unchallenged possession of Egypt. His immediate problem on his accession was to deal with the Mamlūks, who still dominated much of the country, and the ulama, who had helped him to power. The strength of these two groups rested largely on their control of the agricultural land of Egypt and the revenues arising therefrom. Gradually, between 1805 and 1815, Muḥammad ʿAlī eroded the system of tax farming (*iltizām*) that had diverted most of the revenues to the Mamlūks and other notables, imposed the direct levy of taxes, expropriated the landholders, and carried out a new tax survey. In 1809 he divided and outmaneuvered the ulama, and in 1811 he lured many of the Mamlūk leaders to a celebration at the citadel, where he had them massacred. Ibrāhīm expelled their survivors from Upper Egypt, effectively destroying them as a political force.

Muḥammad ʿAlī thus became effectively the sole landholder in Egypt, with a monopoly over trade in crops, although later in his reign he made considerable grants of land to his family and dependents. The monopoly system was extended in due course from primary materials to manufactures, with the establishment of state control over the textile industry. Muḥammad ʿAlī's ambitious hopes of promoting an industrial revolution in Egypt were not realized, fundamentally because of the lack of available sources of power. The monopolies were resented by European merchants in Egypt and clashed with the economic doctrine of free trade upheld by the British government. Although a free-trade convention that was concluded between Britain and the Ottoman Empire in 1838 (the Convention of Balta Liman) was technically binding on Egypt, Muḥammad ʿAlī succeeded in evading its application up to and even after the reversal of his fortunes in 1840–41.

The old-style military forces (including the Albanians) on whom Muḥammad ʿAlī relied against his internal opponents and who conquered the Hejaz, Najd, and the Sudan were heterogeneous and unruly. An attempt to introduce Western methods of training in 1815 provoked a mutiny. Muḥammad ʿAlī then decided to form an army of slave troops dependent wholly upon himself and trained by European instructors. The conquest of the Sudan was intended to provide the recruits. But the slaves, encamped at Aswān, died wholesale, and Muḥammad ʿAlī had to seek most of his troops elsewhere. In 1823 he took the momentous step of conscripting Egyptian peasants for the rank and file of his "new model army." On the other hand, the officers were mostly Turkish-speaking Ottomans, while the director of the whole enterprise, Sulaymān Pasha (Col. Joseph Sève), was a former French officer. The conscription was brutally administered and military life harsh. There were several ineffective peasant revolts, and some potential inductees fled to the towns or to the desert.

As reorganization proceeded, the viceroy gradually built a new administrative structure. While institutions were created and discarded according to his changing needs, Muḥammad ʿAlī depended essentially upon the members of his own family, particularly Ibrāhīm, and loyal servants, such as his Armenian confidant Boghos Bey.

Characteristic of his governmental system were councils of officials, convened to deliberate on public business, and administrative departments (divans) that bore some resemblance to the ministries of European governments. In local administration, Muḥammad ʿAlī established a highly centralized system with a clear chain of command from Cairo through the provincial governors, down to the village headmen. Initiative was not encouraged, but firm control had taken the place of anarchy.

These changes necessitated the training of officers and officials in the new Europeanized ways of working; and this in turn resulted in the creation of a range of educational institutions alongside the traditional Muslim schools that prepared the ulama. Much of the foundation work was done by expatriates, while missions of Egyptian students were sent to Europe, especially to Paris. One of these missions was accompanied by Rifāʿah Rāfiʿ al-Ṭahṭāwī (1801–73), who served as its religious teacher and later played the leading part in inaugurating the translation of European works into Arabic. He thus was a pioneer both in the interpretation of European culture to Egypt and in the renaissance of literary Arabic. The establishment of a government printing press in 1822 facilitated the wide dissemination of the new books.

ʿAbbās I and Saʿīd, 1848–63

The reign of ʿAbbās I (1848–54) indicates how precarious was the advance of westernization in Egypt. The effort had already been relaxed in the last decade of Muḥammad ʿAlī's rule, and ʿAbbās showed himself to be a traditionalist. It was typical of his policy that he closed the school of languages and the translation bureau and sent their director, al-Ṭahṭāwī, to virtual exile in the Sudan. The French, who had played so large a part in Muḥammad ʿAlī's reforms, fell into disfavour, and for diplomatic support ʿAbbās turned to their British rivals, whose help was needed against the Ottomans. Although initially ʿAbbās was ostentatiously loyal to the sultan, he resented an attempt made at that time to curtail his autonomy. The British, for their part, managed to enhance their communications with India by winning from ʿAbbās a concession to build a railway from Alexandria to Cairo; the line was completed between 1851 and 1856 and was extended to Suez two years later. Saʿīd (ruled 1854–63), who succeeded on ʿAbbās's mysterious and violent death, inaugurated another reversal of policy. While he lacked Muḥammad ʿAlī's energy and ability, he was not unsympathetic to the Westernizers. To his French friend Ferdinand de Lesseps (who had been a friend to Muḥammad ʿAlī as well) he granted in 1854 a concession for the cutting of a canal across the isthmus of Suez. This embroiled him both with the sultan, whose prerogative had been encroached upon, and the British, whose overland railway route was threatened by the project; a deadlock lasted throughout his reign.

Ismāʿīl, 1863–79

Ismāʿīl, the son of Ibrāhīm Pasha, who succeeded on the death of Saʿīd, displayed some of his grandfather's dynamic energy and enthusiasm for modernization. He lacked caution, however, and his reign ended in catastrophe. From his predecessors he inherited a precarious economy and a burden of debt. The decline in North American cotton exports caused by the American Civil War (1861–65) greatly increased Britain's demand for Egyptian long-staple cotton. This product had been introduced and developed in Muḥammad ʿAlī's time, but its production had languished until the interruption of supplies of American cotton caused a fourfold increase in price during the war years. When peace returned, prices collapsed with disastrous consequences for the Egyptian economy.

In the management of his finances, Ismāʿīl was both extravagant and unwise and laid himself open to unscrupulous exploitation. Ismāʿīl was committed to the Suez Canal project, but he modified the grant in two important respects: by withdrawing the cession of a strip of land from the Nile River to the Suez isthmus, along which a freshwater canal was to be constructed, and by refusing to provide unlimited (and largely unpaid) peasant labour for the project, a practice that had stirred great outcry in England and continental Europe. The matter was submitted to arbitration; a large indemnity was imposed on Ismāʿīl, who also agreed to pay for a large block of shares put by de Lesseps into Saʿīd's account. French pressure on the sultan succeeded at last in overcoming resistance to the canal project at Constantinople, and a *firman* (decree from the sultan) authorizing its construction was granted in March 1866. Work had in fact already been going on for seven years, and in November 1869 the Suez Canal was opened to shipping by the empress Eugénie, the wife of Napoleon III of France. The incident symbolized the political and cultural orientation of Egypt in the middle decades of the 19th century.

Ismāʿīl, in other ways, presented himself as the ruler of a new and important state. Although his relations with his suzerain, Sultan Abdülaziz (ruled 1861–76), were normally friendly, he was no less eager than his predecessors to secure the autonomy of his dynasty. In 1866 he obtained a *firman* establishing the succession by primogeniture in his own line—abandoning the contemporary Ottoman rule of succession by the eldest male. A year later a *firman* conferred upon Ismāʿīl the special title of khedive, which had in fact been used unofficially since Muḥammad ʿAlī's time and which distinguished the viceroy of Egypt from other Ottoman governors. A period of strained relations developed between the khedive and the sultan arising from

Ismāʿīl's implied pretensions to sovereignty at the time of the opening of the Suez Canal in 1869, but the two were later reconciled; a *firman* reconfirmed the khedive's privileges in 1873. These concessions by the sultan, however, cost Ismāʿīl heavy expenditure—in bribes to Ottoman officials in Constantinople—and an increase in the annual Egyptian tribute and were another factor in the growth of Ismāʿīl's indebtedness.

Ismāʿīl had inherited an African empire in the northern area of the Sudan. Since the middle of the century, in consequence of the abolition of the monopolies, merchants had penetrated south and southwest, up the White Nile and the Al-Ghazāl rivers, in search of ivory. An ancillary slave trade that had developed distressed Europeans, who forgot that their depredations against Africans had continued virtually unabated until the early 19th century, and they prevailed on the khedive to abolish this commerce. Thus, acting on humanitarian and expansionist motives, Ismāʿīl sought to extend Egyptian rule into these remoter regions. He made considerable use of expatriates, notably two Englishmen: explorer Sir Samuel White Baker and military man Sir Charles George ("Chinese") Gordon, who extended the khedive's nominal authority to the African Great Lakes. Another series of events led to the conquest in 1874 of the sultanate of Darfur in the west. The khedive also wished to make Egypt the dominant power in the Red Sea region. The sultan granted him the old Ottoman ports of Sawākin and Mitsiwa in 1865. Egyptian control was established on the Somali coast, and in 1875 the city of Hārer was captured. Attempts to invade Abyssinia in 1875 and 1876 were, however, unsuccessful and marked the limits of Ismāʿīl's imperial expansion.

Like other parts of the Ottoman Empire, Egypt was bound by the capitulations—a system of privileges derived from earlier Western treaties with former sultans. Under the capitulations, European and American residents in Egypt were exempt from local taxation and were subject only to their own consular courts. By patient negotiations over several years, Nūbār Pasha, Ismāʿīl's Armenian minister, succeeded in establishing the Mixed Courts in 1875. These had jurisdiction in civil cases involving Egyptians and foreigners, or foreigners of different nationalities, and had both foreign and Egyptian judges, who administered codes based on French law.

By that time the social consequences of the agrarian and political changes inaugurated by Muḥammad ʿAlī were clearly appearing. The khedive and his family were Egypt's principal landholders, possessing extensive personal estates quite apart from the state lands. Around the khedivial family was a parvenu aristocracy that held the principal civil and military offices. Many of its members were also great landowners; most of them were Turkish or Circassian by origin. Although the peasantry's condition had been harmed by military conscription, by corvées for public works (including large-scale demands for labour on the railways and the Suez Canal), and by ill-considered economic and industrial experiments, the rights of cultivators on their land gradually increased. The richer peasants, from whom the village headmen were recruited, in particular increased in importance. When, in November 1866, Ismāʿīl set up the consultative council known as the Assembly of Delegates, the members of which were chosen by indirect election, the great majority of those elected were village headmen. While Ismāʿīl did not intend to give any of his powers to the Assembly, its establishment and composition pointed to the political growth that would occur among native Egyptians in the next 60 years. Conscription had affected the makeup of the army. The power of the entrenched Turco-Circassians was challenged by native

Egyptian officers, who resented the privileges of their foreign colleagues. The defeat of the Circassian commander in chief, Rātib Pasha, by the Abyssinians in 1876 was a blow from which the prestige of the old officer group never recovered.

From the Assembly, the army, and the westernized intelligentsia emerged politically conscious individuals and groups who drew their ideas from both Western and Islamic sources. Their organization was for the most part small-scale and ephemeral, and their outlook was subversive, being hostile to the autocracy of the khedive, the dominance of the Turco-Circassians, and the pervasive power of the Europeans.

Political tension increased in the last years of Ismāʿīl's reign. Various expedients to postpone bankruptcy (e.g., the khedive's sale in 1875 of his Suez Canal shares to Britain) had failed, and in 1876 the Caisse de la Dette Publique (Commission of the Public Debt) was established for the service of the Egyptian debt. Its members were nominated by France, Britain, Austria, and Italy. In the same year, Egyptian revenue and expenditure were placed under the supervision of a British and a French controller (the Dual Control). After an international enquiry in 1878, Ismāʿīl accepted the principle of ministerial responsibility for government and authorized the formation of an international ministry under Nūbār that included the British and French controllers in his cabinet. Ismāʿīl, however, was not willing to give up his autocracy. In 1879 he exploited an army demonstration against the European ministers to dismiss Nūbār, and he worked in alliance with the Assembly of Delegates to destroy international control over Egypt. By this time, however, his standing outside Egypt had been lost; and in June 1879, Sultan Abdülhamid II (ruled 1876–1909), instigated by France and Britain, deposed him in favour of his son, Muḥammad Tawfīq.

Renewed European Intervention, 1879–82

European domination was immediately reasserted. The Dual Control was revived, with administrator and diplomat Evelyn Baring serving as the British controller. By the Law of Liquidation (July 1880), the annual revenues were divided into two approximately equal portions, one of which was assigned to the Caisse de la Dette, the other to the Egyptian government. The Assembly of Delegates was dissolved. The forces of resistance that Ismāʿīl had stimulated were not, however, allayed by these means. There had already come into existence a nationalist group within the Assembly, prominent among whom was Muḥammad Sharīf, prime minister from April to August 1879. In the army a group of Egyptian officers, whose leader was Aḥmad ʿUrābī (Arabi), was disaffected from the khedive and resentful of European control of Egypt. By 1881 these two groups had allied to form what was called the National Party (al-Ḥizb al-Waṭanī).

Tension surfaced when a petition was presented in January 1881 by ʿUrābī and two of his colleagues against the war minister, ʿUthmān Rifqī, a Circassian. They were arrested and court-martialed but were later set free by mutineers. Tawfīq gave in, dismissed Rifqī, and appointed Maḥmūd Sāmī al-Bārūdī Pasha, one of ʿUrābī's allies, as war minister. But the ʿUrābists still feared reprisals; a military demonstration in Cairo in September 1881 forced Tawfīq to appoint a new ministry under Sharīf and to convene a new Assembly. But the alliance between the officers and Sharīf was uneasy.

Meanwhile, the European powers were becoming increasingly alarmed. A joint English and French note sent in January 1882 with the intention of strengthening the khedive against his opponents had the opposite effect. The Assembly of Delegates swung toward the 'Urābists. Sharīf resigned and al-Bārūdī became premier with 'Urābī as war minister. Rioting ensued on June 11 after British and French naval forces had been sent to Alexandria. From this point Britain took the initiative. The French refused to join in a bombardment of Alexandria (July 11), while an international conference held at Constantinople was boycotted by the Ottomans and produced no solution of the problem. The British government finally resolved to intervene, having secured Tawfīq's support, and sent an expeditionary force under field marshall Sir Garnet Wolseley to the Suez Canal. The 'Urābists were soundly defeated at Tall al-Kabīr (Sept. 13, 1882) by Wolseley's swift surprise attack, and Cairo was occupied the next day.

THE PERIOD OF BRITISH DOMINATION (1882–1952)

The British occupation marked the culmination of developments that had been at work since 1798: the de facto separation of Egypt from the Ottoman Empire, the attempt of European powers to influence or control the country, and the rivalry of France and Britain for ascendancy in the country. Because of the last-minute withdrawal of the French, the British had secured the sole domination of Egypt. The liberal government of British prime minister William Ewart Gladstone was, however, reluctant to prolong the occupation or to establish formal political control, fearing doing so would antagonize both the sultan and the other European powers. That said, the British were unwilling to evacuate Egypt without securing their strategic interests, and this never seemed possible without maintaining a military presence there.

The British Occupation and the Protectorate (1882–1922)

An incident at the outset of the occupation was a particular sign of future tensions. On British insistence, the khedive's government was obliged to place ʿUrābī and his associates on public trial and then to commute the resulting death sentences to exile. Tawfīq's prestige, slight enough at his accession, and diminished in the three years before the occupation, was still further undermined by this intervention of the British government. Meanwhile, Lord Dufferin, the British ambassador in Constantinople, visited Egypt and prepared a report on measures to be taken for the reconstruction of the administrative system. The projects of reform that he envisaged would necessitate an indefinite continuation of the occupation. The implications of this for British policy were slowly and reluctantly accepted by the ministry in London, under pressure from its representative in Cairo, the British agent and consul general, Sir Evelyn Baring, who in 1892 became Lord Cromer.

Two principal problems confronted the occupying power: first, the acquisition of some degree of international recognition for its special but ambiguous position in Egypt, and second, a definition of its relationship to the khedivial government, which formed the official administration of the country. The main European opponents of recognition of the British position were the French, who resented the abolition of the Dual Control (December 1882). The Caisse de la Dette continued to exist, and until 1904 the British had to set their policies to deal with French opposition in this institution. In the early years of the occupation, when Egyptian finances were in disarray, French hostility posed an obstacle, but from 1889 onward there was a budget surplus and consequently greater freedom of action for the Egyptian government. A moderate degree of international agreement over Egypt was attained by the Convention of London (1885), which secured an international loan for the Egyptian government and added two further members (nominated by Germany and Russia) to the Caisse de la Dette. In 1888 the Convention of Constantinople (Istanbul) provided that the Suez Canal should always be open to ships of all countries, in war and peace alike. This was, however, a statement of principle rather than fact; without British cooperation it remained a dead letter.

In matters concerning Egypt's international status, the decisions were made in London, but where the internal administration of the country was concerned, Cromer usually set the policies. Although throughout the occupation the facade of khedivial government was retained, British advisers attached to the various ministries were more influential than were their ministers, while Cromer himself steadily increased his control over the whole administrative machine.

Tawfīq himself gave little trouble, but his prime ministers were more tenacious. Sharīf, premier at the beginning of the occupation until 1884, and his successors, Nūbār Pasha (1884–88) and Muṣṭafa Riyāḍ (Riaz) Pasha (1888–91), resigned because of clashes over administrative control. From then until November 1908, with a break in 1893–95, the prime minister was Muṣṭafā Fahmī Pasha, who proved to be Cromer's obedient instrument.

ʿAbbās Ḥilmī II, 1892–1914

The death of Tawfīq and the accession of his 17-year-old son, ʿAbbās II (Ḥilmī), in 1892 opened a new phase of opposition to the occupation. The new khedive would not submit to Cromer's tutelage, while the British agent resented the attempts of one so much his junior to play a serious role in Egyptian politics. 'Abbās dismissed Muṣṭafā Fahmī in January 1893 and tried to appoint his own nominee as prime minister. Cromer, backed by the British government, frustrated these endeavours, and Fahmī eventually returned to office. 'Abbās provoked another crisis in January 1894 by publicly criticizing British military officers, especially Horatio Herbert Kitchener, the sirdar (commander in chief). Once again Cromer stepped in and forced 'Abbās to make a public apology.

Other considerations apart, the behaviour of 'Abbās in the early years of his reign indicated the emergence of a new generation who had only been children when the occupation began. One of 'Abbās's contemporaries was Muṣṭafā Kāmil (1874–1908), who had studied in France and come to know a group of writers and politicians opposed to the British occupation. On returning to Egypt in 1894, he had reached an understanding with the khedive on the basis of their common opposition to the British occupation. By his speeches and writings (in 1900 he founded his own newspaper, *al-Liwā*), Muṣṭafā Kāmil endeavoured to create an Egyptian patriotism that would rally the entire nation around the khedive. A boost was given to nationalism by the campaigns for the reconquest of the Sudan (1896–98)—to which Egypt provided most of the money and troops, although the commanding officers were British—and by the 1899 Anglo-Egyptian Condominium Agreements, which nominally gave Egypt and Britain joint responsibility for the administration of the reconquered territory but in effect made the Sudan a British possession.

A final episode in the reconquest of the Sudan, the confrontation of British and French at Fashoda on the White Nile in 1898 (the Fashoda Incident), was followed by the reconciliation of the two powers in the Entente Cordiale (1904), which, among other things, gave Britain a free hand in Egypt. This deflated the hopes of Muṣṭafā Kāmil and his alliance with the khedive, who became more willing to cooperate with Cromer. Muṣṭafā Kāmil now turned to Sultan Abdülhamid. When a dispute (the Tābah Incident, 1906) arose between the Ottomans and the occupying power over the Sinai Peninsula, Muṣṭafā Kāmil sought to rally Egyptian nationalist opinion in favour of the sultan, but some Egyptians accused him of harming their national interest in order to favour Islamic unity.

British domination in Egypt and Cromer's personal ascendancy never seemed more secure than in the period following the Entente Cordiale. But the "veiled protectorate" had hidden weaknesses. Cromer was both out of touch and out of sympathy with the new generation of Egyptians. The occupation had become to all intents and purposes permanent, and the consequent growth of the British official establishment frustrated educated Egyptians, who sought government posts for themselves and their sons. The British, however, saw themselves as the benefactors of the Egyptian peasantry, whom they had delivered from the corvée and the lash. The Dinshaway Incident showed them in another light. In June 1906 a fracas between villagers at Dinshaway and a party of British officers out pigeon shooting resulted in the death of a British officer. The special tribunal set up to try the matter imposed exemplary and brutal sentences on the villagers. In the bitter aftermath of this affair, which strengthened Mus.t.afā Kāmil's nationalists, Cromer retired in May 1907.

Sir Eldon Gorst, who succeeded Cromer, had served in Egypt from 1886 to 1904 and brought a fresh mind to bear on the problems of the occupation. He reached an understanding with the khedive and sought to diminish the growing power and numbers of the British establishment. At the same time, he tried to give more effective authority to Egyptian political institutions. Muṣṭafā Fahmī's long premiership ended, and he was followed by a Copt,

Dinshaway Incident

The Dinshaway (or Denshawai) Incident refers to a confrontation in 1906 between residents of the Egyptian village of Dinshaway (Dinshawāy) and British officers during the British occupation of Egypt. Harsh punishments dealt to a number of villagers in the wake of the incident sparked an outcry among many Egyptians and helped galvanize Egyptian nationalist sentiment against British occupation.

In June 1906 a group of British officers agitated the residents of Dinshaway by hunting for sport the pigeons that served as a local source of livelihood. A scuffle broke out, and in the midst of the fray an officer's gun was fired, wounding a female villager and provoking further attack upon the soldiers. An officer who managed to escape the scene fled back toward the British camp on foot in the intense noontime heat; he later collapsed outside the camp and died, likely of heatstroke. A villager who came upon him there tried to assist him, but, when other soldiers from the camp discovered the villager alongside the body of the dead officer, they assumed he had killed him. The villager in turn was killed by the soldiers.

In response to the events at Dinshaway, the British authorities set up a special tribunal to try the villagers for the death of the British officer. The prosecution accused the villagers of premeditated murder, while the defense, among whom was notable Egyptian lawyer and political figure Aḥmad Luṭfī al-Sayyid, claimed that the villagers' actions had been a spontaneous response to the circumstances of the moment. A swift and summary trial found the villagers guilty; they were subsequently given exemplary punishments, ranging from lashes to execution, that were to be carried out publicly at Dinshaway.

The imbalance and severity of the trial proceedings and the punishments that followed were met with reproach in Great Britain and sparked a widespread emotional outpouring among Egyptians that was captured in numerous newspaper articles, essays, and poems. The events at Dinshaway also provided a nexus around which Muṣṭafā Kāmil and other nationalists were able to rally against British occupation.

Buṭrus Ghālī. When a 50-year-old Gorst died prematurely in July 1911, he had attained only limited success. Many British officials resented his policies, which at the same time failed to conciliate the nationalists. Muṣṭafa Kāmil had died in 1908 and had been succeeded by Muḥammad Farīd, who led the National Party toward greater extremism in its opposition to the British. A project to extend the Suez Canal Company's 99-year concession by 40 years was thrown out by the General Assembly (a quasi-parliamentary body, set up in 1883), while Buṭrus Ghālī, who had advocated it, was assassinated a few days later by a nationalist. The appointment of Lord Kitchener to succeed Gorst portended the end of conciliation of the khedive. But Kitchener, although autocratic, was not wholly conservative; his attempts to limit the power and influence of ʿAbbās served the interests of the moderate Egyptians who did not belong to the National Party. The Organic Law of 1913 created a new and more powerful Legislative Assembly that served as a training ground for the nationalist leaders of the postwar period. At the same time, the peasants were helped by improved irrigation and by legal protection of their landholdings from seizure for debt.

World War I and Independence

In November 1914 Britain declared war on the Ottoman Empire. The following month the British proclaimed a protectorate over Egypt, deposed ʿAbbās, and appointed ʿAbbās's uncle, Ḥusayn Kāmil, with the title of sultan. Kitchener was succeeded by Sir Henry McMahon, and he by Sir Reginald Wingate, both with the title of high commissioner. Although Egypt did not have to provide troops, the people, especially the peasantry, suffered from the effects of war. The declaration of martial law and the suspension of the Legislative Assembly temporarily silenced the nationalists. Ḥusayn Kāmil died in October 1917 and was succeeded by his ambitious brother, Aḥmad Fu'ād.

On Nov. 13, 1918, two days after the Armistice, Wingate was visited by three Egyptian politicians headed by Sa'd Zaghlūl, who demanded autonomy for Egypt and announced his intention of leading a delegation (Arabic *wafd*) to state his case in England. The British government's refusal to accept a delegation, followed by the arrest of Zaghlūl, produced a widespread revolt in Egypt; Sir Edmund Henry Hynman Allenby (later Lord Allenby), the victor over the Ottomans in Palestine, was sent out as special high commissioner. Allenby insisted on concessions to the nationalists, hoping to reach a settlement. Zaghlūl was released and subsequently led his delegation to the Paris Peace Conference (1919–20), where it was denied a hearing to plead for Egypt's independence. The Wafd, in the meanwhile, had become a countrywide organization that dominated Egyptian politics. The Milner Commission (1919–20), sent to report on the establishment of constitutional government under the protectorate, was boycotted, but Lord Alfred Milner, who headed the commission, later had private talks with Zaghlūl in London. Finally, hoping to outmaneuver Zaghlūl and to build up a group of pro-British politicians in Egypt, Allenby pressed his government to promise independence without previously securing British interests by a treaty. The declaration of independence (Feb. 28, 1922) ended the protectorate but, pending negotiations, reserved four matters to the British government's discretion: the security of imperial communications, defense, the protection of foreign interests and of minorities, and the Sudan. On March 15 the sultan became King Fu'ād I (ruled 1922–36) of Egypt.

Sa'd Zaghlūl, c. *1920*. Popperfoto/Getty Images

The Kingdom of Egypt (1922–52)

The new kingdom was in form a constitutional monarchy. The constitution, based on that of Belgium and promulgated in April 1923, defined the king's executive powers and established a bicameral legislature. An electoral law provided for universal male suffrage and the indirect election of deputies to the Assembly; the Senate was half elected and half appointed. But Egyptian constitutionalism proved as illusory as Egyptian independence. A political struggle was continually waged among three opportunist contestants—the king, the Wafd, and the British.

The Interwar Period

Never popular, Fu'ād felt insecure and was therefore prepared to intrigue with the nationalists or with the British to secure his position and powers. The Wafd, with its mass following, elaborate organization, and (until his death in 1927) charismatic leader Zaghlūl, was Egypt's only truly national party. Ideologically, it stood for national independence against British domination and for constitutional government against royal autocracy. In practice—and increasingly as time went on—its leaders were prepared to make deals with the British or the king to obtain or retain power. Personal and political rivalries led to the formation of splinter parties, the first of which, the Liberal Constitutionalist Party, broke off as early as 1922. The primary aim of the British government, represented by its high commissioner (after 1936, its ambassador), was to secure imperial interests, especially the control of communications through the Suez Canal. The need for a treaty to safeguard these interests led Britain on more than one occasion to conciliate nationalist feeling by supporting the Wafd against the king.

The first general election, in January 1924, gave the Wafd a majority, and Zaghlūl became prime minister for a few months marked by unsuccessful treaty discussions with the British and tension with the king. When in November 1924 Sir Lee Stack, the sirdar and governor-general of the Sudan, was assassinated in Cairo, Allenby immediately presented an ultimatum that, though later modified by the British government, caused Zaghlūl to resign. The general election of March 1925 left the Wafd still the strongest party, but the parliament no sooner met than it was dissolved. For more than a year Egypt was governed by decree. The third general election, in May 1926, again gave the Wafd a majority. The British opposed a return of Zaghlūl to the premiership, and the office went instead to the Liberal Constitutionalist ʿAdlī Yakan, while Zaghlūl held the presidency of the Chamber of Deputies until his death in 1927. Once again, tension developed between the parliament and the king, and in April 1927 ʿAdlī resigned, to be succeeded by another Liberal Constitutionalist, ʿAbd al-Khāliq Tharwat (Sarwat) Pasha, who negotiated a draft treaty with the British foreign secretary. The draft treaty, however, failed to win the approval of the Wafd. Tharwat resigned in March 1928, and Muṣṭafā al-Naḥḥās Pasha, Zaghlūl's successor as head of the Wafd, became prime minister. But the king dismissed him in June and dissolved the parliament in July. In effect, the constitution was suspended, and Egypt was again governed by decree under a Liberal Constitutionalist premier, Muḥammad Maḥmūd Pasha.

Draft treaty proposals were agreed upon in June 1929, but because Maḥmūd could not overcome Wafdist opposition, Britain pressed for a return to constitutional government, hoping that a freely elected parliament would approve the proposals. In the fourth general election

(December 1929), the Wafd won a majority, and al-Naḥḥās again became premier. Treaty negotiations resumed but broke down over the issue of the Sudan, from which the Egyptians had been virtually excluded since 1924. Al-Naḥḥās also clashed with the king, whose influence he sought to curtail. He resigned in June 1930, and Fu'ād appointed Ismā'īl Ṣidqī Pasha to the premiership. The constitution of 1923 was abrogated, replaced by another promulgated by royal decree. This, with its accompanying electoral law, strengthened the king's power. By this and other measures, Ṣidqī sought to break the power of the Wafd, which boycotted the general election of June 1931. The strong government of Ṣidqī lasted until September 1933, when the king dismissed him. For the next two years palace-appointed governments ruled Egypt.

But Fu'ād, whose health was failing, could not hold out indefinitely against the internal pressure of the Wafd and the external pressure of Britain, which increasingly wanted a treaty with Egypt negotiated specifically through the Wafd. In 1935 the constitution of 1923 was restored, and a general election in May 1936 gave the Wafd a majority once more. Fu'ād had died in the previous month and was succeeded by his son Fārūq I (ruled 1936–52), who was still a minor when he ascended the throne. Al-Naḥḥās became prime minister for the third time. Agreement was quickly reached with Britain, and the Anglo-Egyptian Treaty, a document calling for mutual defense and alliance between the two countries, was signed in August 1936. At the conference in Montreux, Switz., held in the following year, Egypt, backed by Britain, obtained the immediate abolition of the capitulations and the extinction of the Mixed Courts after 12 years. Also in 1937, Egypt became a member of the League of Nations.

Al-Naḥḥās had reached the height of his power, but only briefly. In July 1937 the young king Fārūq came of age and assumed his full royal powers. Popular, with ambitions to rule, Fārūq soon turned against his prime minister. A split developed in the Wafd: Maḥmūd Fahmī al-Nuqrāshī Pasha and Aḥmad Māhir Pasha were expelled and formed the Sa'dist Party. The Wafdist youth movement, known as the Blueshirts, fought with the Greenshirts of Young Egypt, an ultranationalist organization. In December 1937 King Fārūq dismissed al-Naḥḥās. In the ensuing general election (April 1938), the Wafd won only 12 seats.

World War II and Its Aftermath

Although Egypt provided facilities for the British war effort during World War II (1939–45) in accordance with the 1936 treaty, few Egyptians backed Britain and many expected its defeat. In 1940 the British brought pressure on the king to dismiss his prime minister, 'Alī Māhir, and to appoint a more cooperative government. When, early in 1942, German forces threatened to invade Egypt, a second British intervention—often termed the 4 February Incident—compelled King Fārūq to accept al-Naḥḥās as his prime minister. The Wafd, its power confirmed by overwhelming success in the general election of March 1942, cooperated with Britain. Nevertheless, Britain's February intervention had disastrous consequences. It confirmed Fārūq's hostility to both the British and al-Naḥḥās and tarnished the Wafd's pretensions as the standard-bearer of Egyptian nationalism. The Wafd was weakened also by internal rivalries and allegations of corruption.

Al-Naḥḥās was dismissed by the king in October 1944. His successor, Aḥmad Māhir, was acceptable to the British, but he was assassinated in February 1945, at the moment Egypt declared war on Germany and Japan. He was succeeded by a fellow Sa'dist, al-Nuqrāshī.

At the end of World War II, Egypt was in a thoroughly unstable condition. The Wafd declined and its political

Muslim Brotherhood

The Muslim Brotherhood (Arabic: al-Ikhwān al-Muslimūn) is a religio-political organization founded in 1928 at Ismailia, Egypt, by Ḥasan al-Bannā'. Advocating a return to the Qur'ān and the Hadith as guidelines for a healthy, modern Islamic society, the Brotherhood spread rapidly throughout Egypt, the Sudan, Syria, Palestine, Lebanon, and North Africa. Although figures of Brotherhood membership are variable, it is estimated that at its height in the late 1940s it may have had some 500,000 members.

Initially centred on religious and educational programs, the Muslim Brotherhood was seen as providing much-needed social services, and in the 1930s its membership grew swiftly. In the late 1930s the Brotherhood began to politicize its outlook, and, as an opponent of Egypt's ruling Wafd party, during World War II it organized popular protests against the government. An armed branch organized in the early 1940s was subsequently linked to a number of violent acts, including bombings and political assassinations, and it appears that the armed element of the group began to escape Ḥasan al-Bannā''s control. The Brotherhood responded to the government's attempts to dissolve the group by assassinating Prime Minister Maḥmūd Fahmī al-Nuqrāshī in December 1948. Ḥasan al-Bannā' himself was assassinated shortly thereafter; many believe his death was at the behest of the government.

With the advent of the revolutionary regime in Egypt in 1952, the Brotherhood retreated underground. An attempt to assassinate Egyptian Pres. Gamal Abdel Nasser in Alexandria on Oct. 26, 1954, led to the Muslim Brotherhood's forcible suppression. Six of its leaders were tried and executed for treason, and many others were imprisoned. In the 1960s and '70s the Brotherhood's activities remained largely clandestine.

In the 1980s the Muslim Brotherhood experienced a renewal as part of the general upsurge of religious activity in Islamic countries. The Brotherhood's new adherents aimed to reorganize society and government according to Islamic doctrines, and they were vehemently anti-Western. An uprising by the Brotherhood in the Syrian city of Ḥamāh in February 1982 was crushed by the government of Ḥafiz al-Assad at a cost of perhaps 25,000 lives. The Brotherhood revived in Egypt and Jordan in the same period, and beginning in the late 1980s it emerged to compete in legislative elections in those countries.

The participation of the Muslim Brotherhood in parliamentary elections in Egypt in the 1980s was followed by its boycott of the elections of 1990, when it joined most of the country's opposition in protesting electoral strictures. Although the group itself remained formally banned, in the 2000 elections Brotherhood supporters running as independent candidates were able to win 17 seats, making it the largest opposition bloc in the parliament. In 2005, again running as independents, the Brotherhood and its supporters captured 88 seats in spite of efforts by Pres. Hosnī Mubārak's administration to restrict voting in the group's strongholds. Its unexpected success in 2005 was met with additional restrictions and arrests, and the Brotherhood opted to boycott the 2008 elections.

opponents took up the nationalist demand for a revision of the treaty of 1936—in particular for the complete evacuation of British troops from Egypt and the ending of British control in the Sudan. Political activity was passing into the hands of radicals. The Muslim Brotherhood, founded in 1928, developed from a mainstream Islamic reformist movement into a militant mass organization. Demonstrations in Cairo became increasingly frequent and violent. The pressure prevented any Egyptian government from settling its two main external problems: the need to revise the treaty with Britain, and the wish to back the Arabs in Palestine. Negotiations with Britain, undertaken by al-Nuqrāshī and (after February 1946) by his successor, Ṣidqī, broke down over the British refusal to rule out eventual independence for the Sudan. Egypt referred the dispute to the United Nations (UN) in July 1947 but failed to win its case.

Until the interwar period neither the Egyptian public nor the politicians had shown much interest in Arab affairs generally; Egyptian nationalism had developed as an indigenous response to local conditions. After 1936, however, Egypt became involved in the Palestine problem, and in 1943–44 it played a leading part in the formation of the Arab League, which opposed the creation of a Jewish state in Palestine. After World War II, Egypt became increasingly committed to the Arab cause in Palestine, but its unexpected and crushing defeat in the first Arab-Israeli war (1948–49), which had been launched with Syria, Iraq, and Jordan in response to the declaration of the State of Israel in May 1948, contributed to disillusionment and political instability. Meanwhile, the Muslim Brotherhood stepped up its violent activities, and al-Nuqrāshī, again prime minister, tried to suppress the organization. Al-Nuqrāshī was assassinated by a member of the organization in December 1948, and the Brotherhood's leader, Ḥasan al-Bannā', was murdered two months later.

The Wafd won the general election in January 1950, and al-Naḥḥās again formed a government. Failing to reach agreement with Britain, in October 1951 he abrogated both the 1936 treaty and the Condominium Agreement of 1899. Anti-British demonstrations were followed by guerrilla warfare against Britain's garrison in the canal zone. British reprisals in Ismailia led to the burning of Cairo on Jan. 26, 1952. Al-Naḥḥās was dismissed, and there were four prime ministers in the ensuing six months.

THE REVOLUTION AND THE REPUBLIC

At mid-century Egypt was ripe for revolution. Political groupings of both right and left pressed for radical alternatives. From an array of contenders for power, it was a movement of military conspirators—the Free Officers led by Col. Gamal Abdel Nasser—that toppled the monarchy in a coup on July 23, 1952. In broad outline, the history of contemporary Egypt is the story of this coup, which preempted a revolution but then turned into a revolution from above. For more than five decades, rule by Free Officers brought just enough progress at home and enhancement of standing abroad to make Egypt an island of stability in a turbulent Middle East.

Muḥammad Naguib, c. 1953. Hulton Archive/Getty Images

The Nasser Regime

The 1952 coup was fueled by a powerful but vague Egyptian nationalism rather than by a coherent ideology. It produced a regime whose initially reformist character was given more precise form by a domestic power struggle and by the necessity of coming to terms with the British, who still occupied their Suez Canal base.

The domestic challenge to Nasser came in February–April 1954 from Maj. Gen. Muḥammad Naguib, an older officer who served as figurehead for the Free Officers and had been president since June 1953, when Egypt officially became a republic. Political parties had been abolished in January of that year. To supplement his power base in the military forces, Nasser drew on the police and on working-class support mobilized by some of the trade unions. The small middle class, the former political parties, and the Muslim Brotherhood all rallied to Naguib. In the end, Naguib was placed under house arrest, and Nasser assumed the premiership. Nasser's triumph meant that the government would thereafter rely on its military and security apparatus coupled with carefully controlled manipulation of the civilian population.

Obscured in the West was Nasser's initial moderation regarding Egypt's key foreign policy challenges—the Sudan, the British presence, and Israel. An agreement signed in February 1953 established a transitional period of self-government for the Sudan, which became an independent republic in January 1956. Prolonged negotiations led to the 1954 Anglo-Egyptian Agreement, under which British troops were to be evacuated gradually from the canal zone. Some Egyptians criticized the treaty from a nationalist perspective, fearing that external events could permit the British to reoccupy the canal bases.

An attempt to assassinate Nasser by a member of the Muslim Brotherhood in October 1954 was used as a pretext to crush that organization. A number of its members were executed and hundreds were imprisoned under brutal conditions. In the decades to come, these incarcerations were to bear bitter fruit as a generation of Brotherhood militants became hardened and drew new conclusions about the nature of the state in Egypt. One of them, a formerly secularist writer and scholar named Sayyid Quṭb who had come late to the Brotherhood, drew upon his prison experience to draft a template for modern

Egyptian Pres. Gamal Abdel Nasser, c. 1960. Stan Wayman/Time & Life Pictures/Getty Images

Islamic holy war that was afterward embraced by a large number of Egypt's Muslim militants.

In retrospect, it is clear that Nasser was a reluctant champion of the Arab struggle against Israel. Domestic development was his priority. A dangerous pattern of violent interactions, however, eventually drew the Egyptians into renewed conflict with Israel. Small groups of Palestinian raiders (fedayeen), including some operating from Egyptian-controlled Gaza, were infiltrating Israel's borders. Early in 1955 the Israeli government began its policy of large-scale retaliation. One such strike—an attack on Gaza in February 1955 that killed 38 Egyptians—exposed the military weakness of the Free Officer regime, which tried, but failed, to buy weapons from Western countries.

In September 1955 Nasser announced that an arms agreement had been signed between Egypt and Czechoslovakia (acting for the Soviet Union). The way to improved Soviet-Egyptian relations had been prepared by Nasser's refusal to join the Baghdad Pact (the Middle East Treaty Organization, later known as the Central Treaty Organization), which had been formed earlier that year by Turkey, Iraq, Iran, Pakistan, and the United Kingdom, with the support of the United States, to counter the threat of Soviet expansion in the Middle East. With the 1955 arms deal, the Soviet Union established itself as a force in the region.

The erosion of Nasser's initially pro-Western orientation hastened when the United States and Britain refused to give Egypt funds they had previously promised for the construction of the Aswan High Dam. Defiantly, Nasser nationalized the Suez Canal Company in July 1956 in order to use its proceeds to finance the dam. Britain and France, major shareholders in the company, were angered by Nasser's actions (France was equally infuriated by

Egyptian aid to the Algerians who were revolting against French rule) and sought to regain control of the canal by an intricate ruse. In collaboration with France and Britain, Israel, which continued to suffer raids by Egyptian-supported guerrillas, attacked Egypt in October. The two European powers then brought in their own troops, claiming to be enforcing a UN peace resolution, and reoccupied the canal zone. Pressure on the invading powers by the United States and the Soviet Union, however, soon ended the so-called Suez Crisis, leaving Nasser, in spite of his military losses, in control of the canal. The following year, Egypt agreed to the placement of a UN Emergency Force (UNEF) in the Sinai Peninsula to act as a buffer between Egyptian and Israeli forces.

Nasser, who, as the sole candidate, had been elected president in June 1956, pursued a more radical line in the ensuing decade. He created the National Union as an instrument of mobilizing the people and launched an ambitious program of domestic transformation, a revolution from above that was paralleled by a drive for Egyptian leadership in the Arab world. Early in 1958 Egypt combined with Syria to form the United Arab Republic (U.A.R.), but Egyptian dominance antagonized many Syrians, and the union was dissolved in bitterness in September 1961 (Egypt retained the name United Arab Republic until 1971). Nasser blamed the secession on Syrian reactionaries, and in direct response he pushed his revolution in Egypt further to the left. The following spring a National Charter proclaimed Egypt's regime to be one of scientific socialism, with a new mass organization, the Arab Socialist Union (ASU), replacing the National Union. Most large manufacturing firms, banks, transport services, and insurance companies were nationalized or sequestered.

Egypt made dramatic domestic gains. In 1950 manufacturing contributed 10 percent to the total national output;

by 1970 that figure had doubled. However, these achievements in industry were not matched in agriculture, and they were further undercut by Egypt's rapid population growth. In a landmark move toward agricultural reform, Nasser enacted a policy in 1952 that limited land ownership to 200 feddans (208 acres [84 hectares]) per person.

Throughout this period the potential military danger from Israel was a constant factor in the calculations of the U.A.R. government. It worked to strengthen ties with the Soviet bloc and to promote cooperation among the Arab states, even though such attempts usually failed. Nasser masked essential Egyptian moderation on the Israeli issue with a militant rhetoric of confrontation in order to preserve his standing in the Arab world.

The failure of the union with Syria had been a blow to Nasser's pan-Arab policy. To regain the initiative, Nasser intervened in 1962–67 on the republican side in Yemen's civil war. This action led the U.A.R. into conflict with Saudi Arabia, which supported the Yemeni royalists, and with the United States, which backed the Saudis. Until then, Nasser had managed to obtain substantial aid from both the Soviet Union and the United States. Owing to congressional opposition to Nasser's policies, U.S. aid was cut off in 1966.

This series of reversals figured prominently in Nasser's decision to abandon his policy of "militant inaction" toward Israel. For 10 years, relative peace on the border with Israel had been maintained precariously by the presence of the UNEF stationed on the Egyptian side. In the Arab summit conferences of 1964 and 1965, Nasser had counseled restraint, but in 1966 events eluded his control. Palestinian incursions against Israel were launched with greater frequency and intensity from bases in Jordan, Lebanon, and, especially, Syria. A radical Syrian regime openly pledged support to the Palestinian guerrilla raids.

On Nov. 13, 1966, an Israeli strike into Jordan left 18 dead and 54 wounded. Taunted openly for hiding behind the UNEF, Nasser felt he had to act. The Egyptian president requested the UNEF's withdrawal from the Sinai border. But that included, as UN Secretary-General U Thant interpreted the order, removing UN troops stationed at Sharm al-Shaykh at the head of the Gulf of Aqaba. Egyptian troops there proceeded to close the gulf to Israeli shipping.

Israel had made it clear that blockading the gulf would be a cause for war. On June 5, 1967, Israel launched what it called a preemptive attack on Egypt, Jordan, and Syria, which led to a short conflict that came to be known as the June (Six-Day) War. Israel's victory over Egypt and its allies was rapid and overwhelming. Within the first hours of the war, all of Egypt's airfields were struck, and most Egyptian planes were demolished on the ground. In the Sinai Peninsula, Egyptian forces were defeated and put to flight. An estimated 10,000 Egyptians died, and the Israelis reached the Suez Canal on June 8. During the war, Israel occupied the entire Sinai Peninsula (along with territories belonging to the other Arab belligerents), and the Suez Canal was closed to traffic. Instead, the waterway became a fortified ditch between the two warring sides.

Egypt was crushed by the loss, all the more because the government media had painted a rosy but misleading picture of Egyptian operations during the opening days of the war. Nasser, humiliated, resigned, but there was a popular outpouring of support, only partially manipulated by the government, for him to remain in office. Regardless, the Nasser era was, in fact, over. Egypt rearmed rapidly and a low-level conflict, later known as the War of Attrition, soon began along the canal with the Israeli army (particularly its air force). In both domestic and foreign affairs, however, Nasser began a turn to the right that his successor, Anwar el-Sādāt, was to accelerate sharply.

The Sādāt Regime

Nasser died on Sept. 28, 1970, and was succeeded by his vice president, Sādāt, himself a Free Officer. Although then viewed as an interim figure, Sādāt soon revealed unexpected gifts for political survival. In May 1971 he outmaneuvered a formidable combination of rivals for power, calling his victory the "Corrective Revolution." Sādāt then used his strengthened position to launch a war with Israel in October 1973, thereby setting the stage for a new era in Egypt's history.

The Sādāt era really began with the October (Yom Kippur) War of 1973. The concerted Syrian-Egyptian attack on October 6 should have come as no surprise, given the continuing tensions along the canal zone (although the War of Attrition had ended shortly before Nasser's death), but the Arab attack caught Israel completely off guard. Egypt held no illusions that Israel could be vanquished. Rather, the war was launched with the diplomatic aim of convincing a chastened, if still undefeated, Israel to negotiate on terms more favourable to the Arabs. Preparation for the war included Sādāt's announcement in July 1972 that nearly all Soviet military advisers would leave Egypt—partly because the Soviets had refused to sell offensive weapons to the Arab countries.

Egypt did not win the war in any military sense. As soon as Israel recovered from the initial shock of Arab gains in the first few days of fighting—and once the United States abandoned its early neutrality and resupplied Israel with a massive airlift of military supplies—the Israelis drove the Egyptians and Syrians back. A cease-fire was secured by the United States while Egyptian troops remained east of the Suez Canal and Israeli forces had crossed over to its western side.

Still, the initial successes in October 1973 enabled Sādāt to pronounce the war an Egyptian victory and to seek an honourable peace. Egyptian interests, as Sādāt saw them, dictated peace with Israel. In spite of friction with his Syrian allies, Sādāt signed the Sinai I (1974) and Sinai II (1975) disengagement agreements that returned the western Sinai and secured large foreign assistance commitments to Egypt. When Israeli inflexibility combined with Arab resistance to slow events, Sādāt made a dramatic journey to Jerusalem on Nov. 19, 1977, to address the Israeli Knesset (parliament). Tortuous negotiations between Egypt and Israel ensued. The climactic meeting in September 1978 of Sādāt, Israeli Prime Minister Menachem Begin, and U.S. Pres. Jimmy Carter at Camp David in Maryland produced a pair of agreements known

The Camp David trio of Egyptian Pres. Anwar el-Sādāt, U.S. Pres. Jimmy Carter, and Israeli Prime Minister Menachem Begin shaking hands at the White House following their signing of the historic Camp David Accords, Sept. 17, 1978. David Hume Kennerly/Getty Images

as the Camp David Accords. Both Sādāt and Begin were awarded the 1978 Nobel Prize for Peace for these negotiations, and on March 26, 1979, the two leaders formally signed the Israeli-Egyptian peace treaty. The agreement provided for peace between Egypt and Israel and set up a framework for resolving the complex Palestinian issue. Its provisions included the withdrawal of Israeli armed forces and civilians from Sinai within three years, the establishment of special security arrangements on the peninsula, the creation of a buffer zone along the Sinai-Israel border to be patrolled by UN peacekeeping forces, and the normalization of economic and cultural relations between the two countries, including the exchange of ambassadors. The status of the Israeli-occupied West Bank and Gaza territories and the issue of Palestinian autonomy were to be negotiated.

Sādāt linked his peace initiative to the task of economic reconstruction, and proclaimed an open-door policy (Arabic: *infitāḥ*), hoping that a liberalized Egyptian economy would be revitalized by the inflow of Western and Arab capital. The peace process did produce economic benefits, notably a vast U.S. aid program, begun in 1975, that exceeded $1 billion annually by 1981.

The Sādāt peace with Israel was not without its costs, however. As the narrowness of the Israeli interpretation of Palestinian autonomy under the Camp David agreement became clear, Sādāt could not convince the Arab world that the accords would ensure legitimate Palestinian rights. Egypt lost the financial support of the Arab states and, shortly after signing the peace treaty, was expelled from the Arab League.

At home, a new constitution promulgated in 1971 significantly increased the power of individual citizens to participate in the political process, and by 1976 laws were instituted permitting the creation of political parties. But democratization of political life did not prove to be an acceptable substitute for economic revitalization. On Jan. 18–19, 1977, demonstrations provoked by economic hardship broke out in Egypt's major cities. Nearly 100 people were killed, and several thousand were either injured or jailed. The removal of the most oppressive features of Nasser's rule, the return in controlled form to a multiparty system, and (at least initially) the Sādāt peace with Israel were all welcomed. But, as Egypt entered the 1980s, the failure to resolve the Palestinian issue and to relieve mass economic hardships, heightened by the widening class gaps, undermined Sādāt's legitimacy. The West failed to notice this until, in September 1981, Sādāt arrested some 1,500 of Egypt's political elite.

Perhaps more ominous during the 1970s were the signs of rising Muslim extremism throughout the country. Under Nasser, the Muslim Brotherhood had been firmly squelched. Sayyid Quṭb had been executed in 1966 for treason, but large numbers of Muslim activists—many of them radicalized by imprisonment and by Quṭb's writings on jihad and the apostasy of modern Muslim culture—went underground. Under Sādāt, groups of Muslim activists were given wide latitude to proselytize, particularly on Egypt's university campuses, where it was hoped that they would counter lingering left-wing and Nasserite sentiment among the students, and members of the Muslim Brotherhood were released from prison and allowed to operate with relative freedom. Yet during that time there was a growing rise in religious violence, particularly directed against the country's Coptic community but also, with growing frequency, against the government. The group al-Takfīr wa al-Hijrah (roughly, "Identification of Unbelief and Flight from Evil"—founded in 1967 after Quṭb's execution) engaged in several terrorist attacks during the decade, and other groups, namely Islamic Jihad (al-Jihād al-Islāmī) and the Islamic Group (al-Jamā'ah al-Islāmiyah), formed with the goal of overthrowing Egypt's secular state.

Egypt After Sādāt

Sādāt's assassination on Oct. 6, 1981, by militant soldiers associated with Islamic Jihad was greeted in Egypt by uprisings in some areas but mostly by a deafening calm. It was with a profound sense of relief that Egyptians brought Hosnī (Ḥusnī) Mubārak, Sādāt's handpicked vice president, to power, with a mandate for cautious change. As an air force general and hero of the October War, Mubārak had worked closely with Sādāt since 1973.

During his first year as president, Mubārak struck a moderate note, neither backing away from the peace with Israel nor loosening ties with the United States. By pursuing that steady course, he was able to prevent any delay in the return of the occupied Sinai Peninsula to Egyptian sovereignty in April 1982. At the same time, Mubārak tried to contain the disaffections that had surfaced in the last year of Sādāt's era. He announced the end of the reign of the privileged minority that had dominated the invigorated private sector during the Sādāt years. He also released Sādāt's political prisoners, while prosecuting vigorously the Islamic militants who had plotted the late president's assassination. Unfortunately, Egypt's worsening economic problems could not be solved quickly. But in his very first speeches Mubārak did frankly and perceptively identify Egypt's economic shortcomings.

These solid beginnings were undercut when Israel invaded Lebanon in June 1982, only five weeks after the Jewish state's final withdrawal from the Sinai Peninsula. In Egypt the invasion was perceived as an Israeli attempt to destroy Palestinian nationalism, and Mubārak was accused by his foes of allowing Israel to exploit Egypt's disengagement. Official relations with Israel were severely strained until Israel initiated its partial withdrawal from Lebanon in 1985. However, Mubārak's cautious policies did enable Egypt to repair its relationships with most of the moderate Arab states. At an Arab League summit in 1987, each government was authorized to restore diplomatic relations with Egypt as it saw fit; Iraq—which had been a leading critic of Sādāt's peace with Israel but by then was in a protracted war with Iran—took that opportunity to purchase military supplies from Egypt. Egypt resumed membership in the league two years later.

Within the country, opposition to a variety of political, economic, and social policies continued, chiefly among discontented labour and religious groups. The government contained labour strikes, food riots, and other incidents of unrest and adopted several measures aimed at curbing a determined drive by Islamic extremists to destabilize the regime.

In the late 1980s Egypt's economy suffered markedly from falling oil prices and was further weakened by a drop in the number of remittances from its three million workers abroad. In spite of a rising debt burden, the government continued to rely heavily on foreign economic aid, leading to growing interference by the International Monetary Fund (IMF) in Egypt's economic policies; in 1991 the Egyptian government signed the Economic Reform and Structural Adjustment Program with the IMF and the World Bank. The country's currency, the Egyptian pound, had to be devalued several times, interest rates were raised, and subsidies were lowered on food and fuel. These policies especially harmed the poorest Egyptians, who often looked to Islamist groups such as the Muslim Brotherhood for assistance. Some Muslim extremists, however, including Islamic Jihad and the Islamic Group, continued to

Hosnī Mubārak

(b. May 4, 1928, Al-Minūfiyah governorate, Egypt)

Hosnī Mubārak (in full, Muḥammad Hosnī Saʿīd Mubārak) has been president of Egypt since October 1981.

Mubārak graduated from the Egyptian military academy at Cairo (1949) and the air academy at Bilbays (1950), receiving advanced flight and bomber training in the Soviet Union. He held command positions in the Egyptian air force and from 1966 to 1969 was director of the air academy. In 1972 Pres. Anwar el-Sādāt appointed Mubārak chief commander of the air force, and in this capacity he was credited with the successful performance of the Egyptian air force in the opening days of the war with Israel in October 1973. He was promoted to the rank of air marshal in 1974. In April 1975 Sādāt named him vice president, and in subsequent years Mubārak was active in most of the negotiations involving Middle Eastern and Arab policy. He served as the chief mediator in the dispute between Morocco, Algeria, and Mauritania over the future of Western (Spanish) Sahara.

Ḥosnī Mubārak, 1982. Barry Iverson/ Gamma

Mubārak became president following Sādāt's assassination on Oct. 6, 1981. His years in office were marked by an improvement in Egypt's relations with the other Arab countries and by a cooling of relations with Israel, especially following the Israeli invasion of Lebanon in 1982. He reaffirmed Egypt's peace treaty with Israel (1979) under the Camp David Accords, however, and cultivated good relations with the United States, which remained Egypt's principal aid donor. In 1987 Mubārak was elected to a second six-year term as president. During the Persian Gulf crisis and war following Iraq's invasion of Kuwait in 1990–91, Mubārak led other Arab states in supporting the Saudi decision to invite the aid of a U.S.-led military coalition to recover Kuwait. He also played an important role in mediating the bilateral agreement between Israel and the Palestine Liberation Organization that was signed in 1993.

Mubārak was reelected president in 1993. He subsequently faced a rise in guerrilla violence and growing unrest among opposition parties, which pressed for democratic electoral reforms (the last free elections in Egypt had been held in 1950). He launched a campaign against Islamic fundamentalists, especially the Islamic Group, which was responsible for a 1997 attack at Luxor that left some 60 foreign tourists dead. In 1995 he escaped an assassination attempt in Ethiopia and in 1999 was slightly wounded after being attacked by a knife-wielding assailant. Throughout, Mubārak continued to press for peace in the Middle East. Running unopposed, he was reelected to a fourth term as president in 1999. In 2005 Mubārak easily won Egypt's first multicandidate presidential election, which was marred by low voter turnout and allegations of irregularities.

U.S. pres. George W. Bush (left) *and Egyptian pres. Hosnī Mubārak meeting in Egypt, Jan. 16, 2008.* Eric Draper/The White House

resort to terrorism against political leaders, secularist writers, Copts, and even foreign tourists, the last-named being a major source of Egypt's foreign exchange.

Politics in Egypt continued to follow authoritarian patterns, as Mubārak was reelected to the presidency without opposition in 1987, 1993, and 1999, and although opposition candidates contested the 2005 election, he was reelected that year as well. His National Democratic Party continued to increase its majority of delegates in the People's Assembly in the elections held every five years. The Muslim Brotherhood, unofficially allowed to revive under Sādāt but never authorized to become a political party, threw its popular support to the New Wafd in one election and to the Liberal Socialists in another. It was widely believed that voting results were rigged to ensure that Mubārak's supporters would win.

Although Egypt's press was freer than it had been under Nasser or Sādāt, Mubārak introduced a law in 1995 that would imprison journalists or party leaders who published news injurious to a government official. Popular pressure caused the Assembly to scale down the law, which was eventually voided by Egypt's Constitutional Court. However, the growing censorship by the Islamic courts and the rector of al-Azhar University tempered freedom of speech and the press in the late 20th and early 21st centuries.

In its struggle against Islamist terrorism, Mubārak's regime resorted to preventive detention and, allegedly, torture. Egyptian terrorists, for their part, assassinated several government ministers, nearly killed Mubārak himself in Addis Ababa, Eth., in 1995, and gunned down tourists near Egypt's most famous monuments—including an especially violent attack at Luxor in 1997. A leading Islamist, Sheikh 'Umar 'Abd al-Raḥmān, escaped to the United States, where he took part in a 1993 truck bomb attack on New York City's World Trade Center and was later sentenced to life imprisonment for that crime and for conspiracy to commit further attacks. Another Islamist leader, a Cairene pediatrician named Ayman al-Zawahiri, fled to Afghanistan, where he led members of Islamic Jihad in joining the transnational terrorist organization known as al-Qaeda. In spite of government initiatives to control the problem, domestic terrorism remains a threat to Egypt's stability.

Some social and economic problems either stemmed from or were exacerbated by Egypt's involvement in the Persian Gulf War (1990–91) on the side of the U.S.-led coalition. Egyptian troops took part in the conflict, as did soldiers from many Arab countries. Although Egypt was rewarded for its participation by forgiveness of billions of dollars that it owed for the purchase of arms from the West, many Egyptian expatriate workers lost their jobs in Iraq because of that country's invasion of Kuwait. Likewise, Egypt's hopes that its contractors would win bids to help rebuild Kuwait after the war were disappointed, and a plan to station Egyptian and Syrian troops as peacekeepers in the region was rejected by the Persian Gulf states. Perhaps understandably, financially strapped Egyptians began to resent wealthy Saudis, Kuwaitis, and other gulf Arabs who often spent their vacations gambling in Cairo's luxury hotels.

The Egyptian public also grew skeptical of ongoing efforts by successive U.S. presidents and by their own president to promote peace between Israel and other Arab countries and, particularly, the Palestinians. In a changing global economy, there was a popular suspicion that such attempts at fostering better relations might have some ulterior motive. In particular, many Egyptians feared a possible U.S. and Israeli attempt to manipulate Egypt's industries, especially since computer and information technology—both of which Egypt depended heavily on the West to obtain and use—became more vital to economic growth. Since 2004, however, expansion of the country's Internet connectivity has ranked particularly high on the economic agenda of Egypt's prime minister, Ahmad Nazif, himself a computer engineer.

In fact, Mubārak's commitment to domestic development was evident in his choice of three successive economic planners to serve as prime minister during the 1990s. And though Egypt was becoming ever more sophisticated economically, it was doing so at a high price. Its independence was being curtailed by interference from international lenders such as the IMF, and a growing disparity in income and access to resources was straining relations between its rich and poor citizens as well as contributing to the erosion of unity between its Muslims and Copts. While some Muslims accused the Copts of serving as agents for foreign powers and of controlling Egypt's economy, some Copts accused Muslims of destroying churches and compelling Egyptian Christians to convert to Islam. Although both Muslim and Christian Egyptians have, for the most part, made an effort to minimize their differences publicly in order to maintain national unity, rapid and uneven development has ultimately posed a threat to Egypt's political and cultural leadership of the Arab world.

CONCLUSION

From ancient times to the present day, the Nile River has been a central factor in Egyptian life. The agrarian population of ancient Egypt depended upon the river's annual inundation for sustenance; fertile land and the general reliability of the river's flood allowed for the storage of surpluses to protect against crop failure and formed the basis of Egyptian prosperity. In modern times—even as the construction of the Aswan High Dam meant that human ingenuity was, for the first time, able to control the river's floodwaters—the Nile remained crucial. Much of the population of modern Egypt is clustered along its banks in areas that bear some of the highest population densities of the world, and Egypt's small proportion of arable land is meticulously harvested. In a country that is more than 95 percent desert, the presence of the Nile has allowed for life—and sustained it—for millennia.

Egypt's strategic location was not lost on the European powers that battled for influence and control there from the late 18th century. France's occupation of Egypt, designed to thwart British interests, was relatively brief; it was nevertheless significant, exerting great change on Egypt's internal politics and inaugurating an era of European influence. It was from the British—who occupied Egypt after the French—that the Egyptian nationalists had to win their freedom, however, and although independence was achieved in 1922, British influence would remain for decades to come. Under Nasser, Egypt confronted both the British and the French over the Suez Canal, the value of which could not be underestimated by either power, both of whom were among the canal's major shareholders. Egypt maintained relatively good relations with the West in subsequent years, however, especially following Pres. Anwar el-Sādāt's mission to Jerusalem to forge a peace agreement with Israel.

In 2005, when Pres. Hosnī Mubārak was elected to his fifth term, Egypt had been governed by a single president since the 1980s and only two others since 1954. At the end of the first decade of the 21st century, it remained to be seen whether Egyptian politics would continue along authoritarian lines, and what balance would be struck between the competing narratives of nationalism, socialism, and Islamism.

GLOSSARY

abrogate Annul; nullify.

alluvium Clay, silt, sand, gravel, or similar detrital material deposited by running water.

anarchic Of, relating to, or advocating anarchy (lawlessness).

apostolic Of, relating to, or conforming to the teachings of the Christian bible apostles.

bey A courtesy title used in Turkey and Egypt.

brackish Somewhat salty.

caliph Muslim ruler.

capitulation In the history of international law, any treaty whereby one state permitted another to exercise extraterritorial jurisdiction over its own nationals within the former state's boundaries. The term is to be distinguished from the military term "capitulation," an agreement for surrender.

caravansary An inn surrounding a court in eastern countries where caravans rest at night.

chamberlain A chief officer in the household of a king or nobleman.

Circassian A member of a group of peoples of the northwestern Caucasus.

citadel A fortress that commands a city.

coking To change into coke, the residue of coal left after destructive distillation and used as fuel.

consort Spouse.

corvée Unpaid labour (as toward constructing roads) due from a feudal vassal to his lord.

dead letter Something that has lost its force or authority without being formally abolished.

dowry In some cultures, the money, goods, or estate that a woman brings to her husband in marriage.

endemic Belonging or native to a particular people or country.

entrepôt An intermediary centre of trade and transshipment.

fastness Remote and secluded place.

fecund Fruitful.

fellah Peasant or agricultural labourer in an Arab country (as Egypt).

fief Something over which one has the right to exercise control.

fortnight Two weeks.

historiography The writing of history; especially: the writing of history based on the critical examination of sources, the selection of particulars from the authentic materials, and the synthesis of particulars into a narrative that will stand the test of critical methods.

indemnity Security against hurt, loss, or damage.

jellaba Known as a gallibiya in Egypt, the garment generally has wide, long sleeves, and the long skirt may be slit up the sides; some styles are open in front like a coat or caftan.

junta A group of persons controlling a government especially after a revolutionary seizure of power.

khedive A ruler of Egypt from 1867 to 1914 governing as a viceroy of the sultan of Turkey.

loanword A word taken from another language and at least partly naturalized.

militate To have weight or effect.

parvenu One who has recently or suddenly risen to an unaccustomed position of wealth or power and has not yet gained the prestige, dignity, or manner associated with it.

physiographic Exterior physical features and changes of the earth.

polemic An aggressive attack on or refutation of the opinions or principles of another.

polyglot Multilingual.

primogeniture An exclusive right of inheritance belonging to the eldest son.

promulgate To make (as a doctrine or constitution) known by open declaration.

riverine Living or situated on the banks of a river.

savant A person of learning, especially one with detailed knowledge in some specialized field.

sirdar Commander of the Anglo-Egyptian army.

sorghum Cereal grain plant of the family Poaceae, probably native to Africa, and its edible starchy seeds.

Sunni One of the two major branches of Islam, the branch that consists of the majority of that religion's adherents. Sunnite Muslims regard their sect as the mainstream and traditionalist branch of Islam, as distinguished from the minority sect, the Shi'ites.

suzerain A dominant state controlling the foreign relations of a vassal state but allowing it sovereign authority in its internal affairs.

Turkoman A member of a Turkic-speaking traditionally nomadic people living chiefly in Turkmenistan, Afghanistan, and Iran.

ulama The learned of Islam, those who possess the quality of 'ilm, "learning," in its widest sense.

vernacular A language or dialect native to a region or country rather than a literary, cultured, or foreign language.

vizier A high executive officer of various Muslim countries and especially of the Ottoman Empire.

wadi The bed or valley of a stream in regions of southwestern Asia and northern Africa that is usually dry except during the rainy season and that often forms an oasis.

BIBLIOGRAPHY

Specialized works on geography include Rushdi Said (ed.), *The Geological Evolution of the River Nile* (1981); Jean Kérisel, *The Nile and Its Masters: Past, Present, and Future: Source of Hope and Anger* (2001), trans. by Philip Cockle; and Bonnie M. Sampsell, *A Traveler's Guide to the Geology of Egypt* (2003). Plants and animals are discussed in Vivi Täckholm, Gunnar Täckholm, and Mohammed Drar, *Flora of Egypt*, 4 vol. (1941–69, reprinted 1973).

Studies on the Egyptian population include Joseph J. Hobbs, *Bedouin Life in the Egyptian Wilderness* (1989), which discusses an Arab tribe living in the Eastern Desert. Anwar G. Chejne, *The Arabic Language: Its Role in History* (1969, reissued 1980), covers the background of classical Arabic. Coverage of Egypt's indigenous Christian population is in Aziz S. Atiya (ed.), *The Coptic Encyclopedia*, 8 vol. (1991). Denis J. Sullivan and Sana Abed-Kotob, *Islam in Contemporary Egypt: Civil Society vs. the State* (1999), discusses the Muslim majority.

Studies of the Egyptian economy include Galal A. Amin, *Whatever Happened to the Egyptians?: Changes in Egyptian Society from 1950 to the Present* (2000); Ibrahim M. Oweiss (ed.), *The Political Economy of Contemporary Egypt* (1990); Phebe Marr (ed.), *Egypt at the Crossroads: Domestic Stability and Regional Role* (1999); John Waterbury, *The Egypt of Nasser and Sadat: The Political Economy of Two Regimes* (1983); and Eberhard Kienle, *A Grand Delusion: Democracy and Economic Reform in Egypt* (2001).

Government and society are covered in Ninette S. Fahmy, *The Politics of Egypt: State-Society Relationship* (2002); and James B. Mayfield, *Local Institutions and Egyptian Rural Development* (1974). Education is the subject of Bayard Dodge, *Al-Azhar: A Millennium of Muslim Learning* (1961, reissued 1974); and Donald Malcolm Reid, *Cairo University and the Making of Modern Egypt* (1990, reissued 2002). Other works on social conditions include Margot Badran, *Feminists, Islam, and Nation: Gender and the Making of Modern Egypt* (1995); Azza M. Karam, *Women, Islamisms, and the State: Contemporary Feminism in Egypt* (1998); and Andrea B. Rugh, *Family in Contemporary Egypt* (1984).

Works dealing with arts and culture include Walter Armbrust, *Mass Culture and Modernism in Egypt* (1996); Joel Gordon, *Revolutionary Melodrama: Popular Film and Civic Identity in Nasser's Egypt* (2002); Virginia Danielson, *The Voice of Egypt: Umm Kulthum, Arabic Song and Egyptian Music in the Twentieth Century* (1997); Roger Allen, *The Arabic Novel: An Historical and Critical Introduction*, 2nd ed. (1995); Salma Khadra Jayyusi and Roger Allen (eds.), *Modern Arabic Drama: An Anthology* (1995); and Liliane Karnouk, *Modern Egyptian Art, 1910–2003*, new rev. ed. (2005), on the visual arts.

Egypt's history since Islam is well covered in Carl F. Petry and M.W. Daly (eds.), *Cambridge History of Egypt*, 2 vol. (1998). Early Muslim Egypt is discussed in Francesco Gabrieli, *Muhammad and the Conquests of Islam*, trans. by Virginia Luling and Rosamund Linell (1968, reissued 2002; originally published in Italian, 1967). Fāṭimid studies have been transformed by S.D. Goitein, *A Mediterranean Society: The Jewish Communities of the Arab World as Portrayed in the Documents of the Cairo Geniza* (1967–88, reissued 1999). Mamlūk and Ottoman Egypt are considered in F.R.C. Bagley (ed. and trans.), *The Last Great Muslim Empires* (1969, reissued 1996), part 3 of *The Muslim World: A Historical Survey*, 3 vol. (1960–69; originally published in German, 1952–59). An account of the early Mamlūk state is found in Robert Irwin, *The Middle East in the Middle Ages: The Early Mamluk Sultanate, 1250–1382* (1986); and the Ottoman period is discussed in Michael Winter, *Egyptian Society Under Ottoman Rule, 1517–1798* (1992).

The relationship between economy and religion in early modern Egypt are described in Peter Gran, *Islamic Roots of Capitalism: Egypt, 1760–1840* (1979, reissued 1998). Political developments of the 19th century are discussed in Ehud R. Toledano, *State and Society in Mid-Nineteenth-Century Egypt* (1990); Afaf Lutfi Al-Sayyid-Marsot, *Egypt in the Reign of Muhammad Ali* (1984); and Khaled Fahmy, *All the Pasha's Men: Mehmed Ali, His Army, and the Making of Modern Egypt* (1997, reissued 2002). Roger Owen, *Lord Cromer: Victorian Imperialist, Edwardian Proconsul* (2004) is also useful. A good survey of Egypt between the 1919 and 1952 revolutions is Selma Botman, *Egypt from Independence to Revolution, 1919–1952* (1991); also useful is Arthur Goldschmidt, Jr., Amy J. Johnson, and Barak A. Salmoni (eds.), *Re-Envisioning Egypt, 1919–1952* (2005). Nasser's revolution is the subject of Joel Gordon, *Egypt's Blessed Movement: Egypt's Free Officers and the July Revolution* (1992); and Kirk J. Beattie, *Egypt During the Nasser Years: Ideology, Politics, and Civil Society* (1994), which examines the dynamics of the Nasser regime. Also useful are Nazih N. Ayubi, *The State and Public Policies in Egypt Since Sadat* (1991); Kirk J. Beattie, *Egypt During the Sadat Years* (2000); and Robert Springborg, *Mubarak's Egypt: Fragmentation of the Political Order* (1989).

INDEX

A

B

C

H

I

J

K

L

M

N

O

P

Q

R

S

T

Tawfīq, Muḥammad, 139, 140, 141, 142, 143
telecommunication, 49, 52–54
television, 54, 75, 89
temperatures, seasonal, 10
terrorism, 167, 172–173
Tharwat Pasha, ʻAbd al-Khāliq, 151
theatre, modern, 75
topography/relief, 1–6
tourism, 47
trade, 46–47, 48
trade unions, 48–49
trading partners, 47
transportation, 48, 49–52
Ṭūlūnid dynasty, 98–101, 102

U

Umayyad caliphate, 92, 95
United Arab Republic (U.A.R.), 56, 161, 162
United States, 39, 45, 47, 63, 160, 161, 162, 164, 165, 166, 168, 171, 172, 173
ʻUrābī, Aḥmad, 140, 142
ʻUthmān Bey al-Bardīsī, 127
ʻUthmān ibn ʻAffān, 96–97

W

Wafd, 148, 150, 151, 152, 153–155, 156
Western Desert, 1, 2, 5–6, 7, 8, 10, 11, 12, 16, 17, 18, 21, 24, 27, 37, 39, 50
White Nile, 8, 9, 137, 144
World Bank, 46
World War I, 75, 147–148
World War II, 41, 45, 46, 65, 66, 153–156

Z

Zaghlūl, Saʻd, 148, 150, 151